Word 2016 Level 1
Student Edition

30 Bird Media
510 Clinton Square
Rochester NY 14604
www.30Bird.com

Word 2016 Level 1

Student Edition

CEO, 30 Bird Media: Adam A. Wilcox

Series designed by: Clifford J. Coryea, Donald P. Tremblay, and Adam A Wilcox

Managing Editor: Donald P. Tremblay

Instructional Design Lead: Clifford J. Coryea

Copyeditor: Robert S. Kulik

Keytester: Kurt J. Specht

COPYRIGHT © 2016 30 Bird Media LLC. All rights reserved

No part of this work may be reproduced or used in any other form without the prior written consent of the publisher.

Visit www.30bird.com for more information.

Trademarks

Some of the product names and company names used in this book have been used for identification purposes only and may be trademarks or registered trademarks of their respective manufacturers and sellers.

Disclaimer

We reserve the right to revise this publication without notice.

WORD2016-L1-R20-SCB

Table of Contents

Introduction 1
    Course setup 2

Chapter 1: Fundamentals 3
    Module A: Getting around 4
    Module B: Creating documents 11
    Module C: Document views 22

Chapter 2: Formatting 27
    Module A: Formatting characters 28
    Module B: Formatting paragraphs 32
    Module C: Quick Styles 46
    Module D: Making lists 51

Chapter 3: Document setup 61
    Module A: Page layout 62
    Module B: Proofing documents 74
    Module C: Printing, headers, and footers 83
    Module D: Templates 93

Chapter 4: Graphics 101
    Module A: Inserting pictures 102
    Module B: Formatting pictures 107
    Module C: Picture layout 112

Chapter 5: Tables 119
    Module A: Creating tables 120
    Module B: Formatting tables 127

Alphabetical Index 135

Introduction

Welcome to *Word 2016 Level 1*. This course provides the basic concepts and skills to start being productive with Microsoft Word 2016: how to create, format, and set up a document, and how to add graphics and tables. This course, and the two that come after, map to the objectives of the Microsoft Office Specialist and Expert exams for Word 2016. Objective coverage is marked throughout the course, and you can download an objectives map for the series from http://www.30bird.com.

You will benefit most from this course if you want to accomplish basic workplace tasks in Word 2016, or if you want to have a solid foundation for continuing on to become a Word Expert. If you intend to take a Microsoft Office Specialist or Expert exam for Word, this course is a good place to start your preparation, but you will need to continue on to other courses in the series to be fully prepared for either exam.

The course assumes you know how to use a computer, and that you're familiar with Microsoft Windows. It does not assume that you've used a different version of Word or another word processing program before.

After you complete this course, you will know how to:

- Create and save documents, cut and paste text, and use different document views
- Format characters and paragraphs; use styles, Quick Styles, and themes; and create bulleted and numbered lists
- Set up page layout, set tab stops, use headers and footers, and apply templates
- Insert, format, and lay out pictures
- Insert and format tables

This is the first course in a series. After you complete it, consider going on to the others:

- *Word 2016: Level 2*
- *Word 2016: Level 3*

Introduction / Course setup

Course setup

To complete this course, each student and instructor will need to have a computer running Word 2016. Setup instructions and activities are written assuming Windows 10; however, with slight modification the course will work using Windows XP Service Pack 3, Windows Vista Service Pack 1, Windows 7 or Windows 8.x.

Hardware requirements for Windows 10 course setup include:

- 1 GHz or faster processor (32- or 64-bit)
- 1 GB (32-bit) or 2 GB (64-bit) RAM
- 25 GB total hard drive space (50 GB or more recommended)
- DirectX 10 (or later) video card or integrated graphics, with a minimum of 128 MB of graphics memory
- Monitor with 1280x800 or higher resolution
- Wi-Fi or Ethernet adapter

Software requirements include:

- Windows 10 (or alternative, as above)
- Microsoft Word 2016 or any Microsoft Office 2016 edition
- The Word 2016 Level 1 data files and PowerPoint slides, available at http://www.30bird.com

Network requirements include:

- An Internet connection to use online templates and images (which can be skipped or demonstrated by the instructor)

Because the exercises in this course include viewing and changing some Word defaults, it's recommended to begin with a fresh installation of the software. But this is certainly not necessary. Just be aware that if you are not using a fresh installation, some exercises might work slightly differently, and some screens might look slightly different.

 Note: Opening downloaded files in Office applications can result in the document being displayed in Protected View. This can be overridden by clicking **Enable Editing** at the top of the document window.

1. Install Windows 10, including all recommended updates and service packs. Use a different computer and user name for each student.
2. Install Microsoft Word 2016 or Office 2016, using all defaults during installation.
3. Update Word or Office using Windows Update.
4. Copy the Word 2016 Level 1 data files to the Documents folder.

Chapter 1: Fundamentals

You will learn how to:

- Get around the Word interface
- Create and save a new document
- View documents in different ways

Module A: Getting around

First thing you'll need to do is start Word. Once you're in, at the top of the screen you'll see a set of tools called the *ribbon*. You'll use commands and buttons on the ribbon and elsewhere to create documents.

You will learn:

- The layout of the Word interface and the ribbon
- About Backstage view
- How to open and close documents

The Word interface

The most prominent feature of the Word 2016 interface is the ribbon. Other features include the Quick Access toolbar, rulers, and the status bar.

The Word 2016 interface

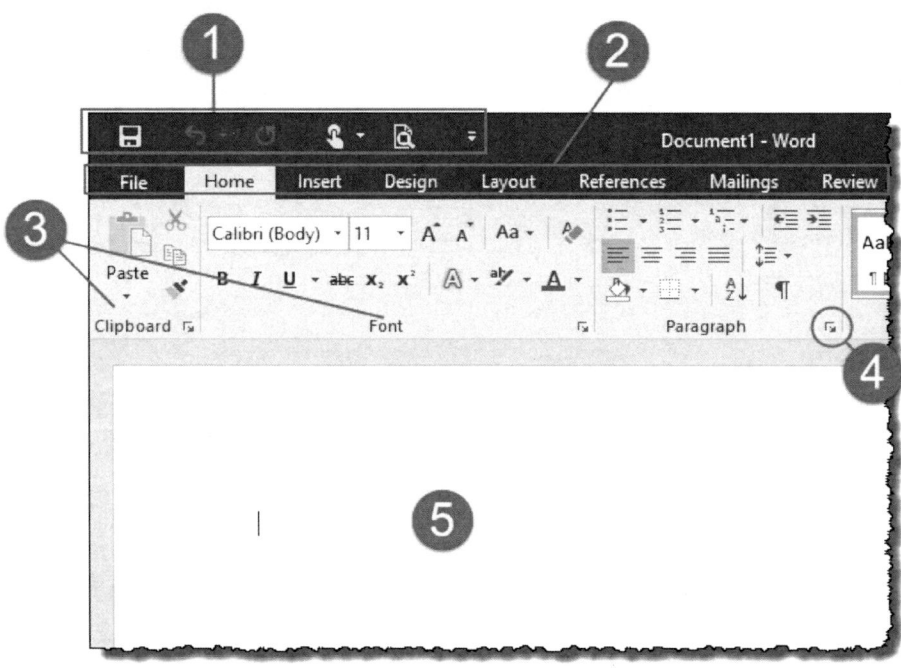

1. The *Quick Access toolbar* holds a few of the commands that you use most.

2. The ribbon *tabs* divide ribbon commands into general categories. Some tabs appear only in certain contexts. For instance, if the cursor is in a table, then table Design and Layout tabs will appear.

3. Ribbon *groups* further divide commands on a tab into logical groupings, like Font and Paragraph. You can hide the groups by clicking ⌃ (the Collapse the Ribbon button) on the right end of the ribbon. The groups are hidden until you click a tab, and remain hidden again until you return to the document.

4. Some ribbon groups have a button in the lower-right corner that opens a window with more options.

5. The *document window* is where you create your documents.

Along the bottom of the Word window you'll see the *status bar*, which shows information such as page number and word count, and the current document view and zoom percentage.

The Word status bar

Starting Microsoft Word 2016

You can start Word from the Start menu, or you can add icons to the desktop or the taskbar. In Windows 10, use of the Start menu is greatly simplified.

1. Move your mouse pointer to the lower-left corner of the screen to display the Windows Start icon.
2. Click **Start**.
   To display the All apps menu.
3. Scroll down to see the Word 2016 icon.
4. Click **Word 2016**.
   The Word startup window opens. Any recent files you've opened appear on the left, and there are tiles for different types of documents you can open on the right.
5. Click **Blank document**.

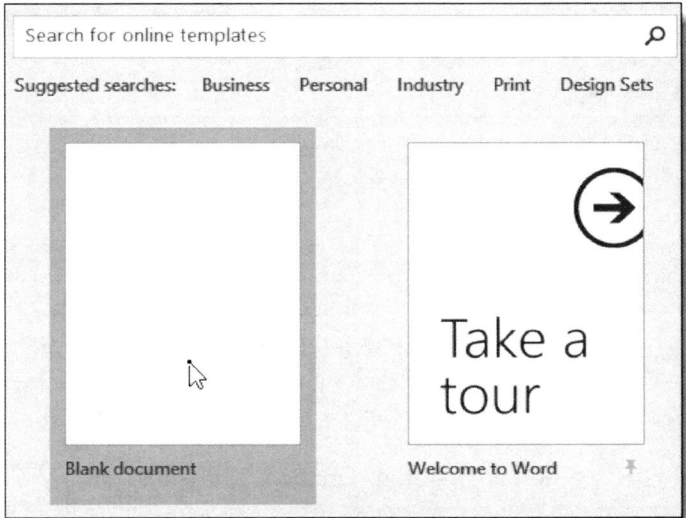

The Word window opens to a blank document.

If you want to pin the Word icon to the taskbar, right-click the icon, and click **Pin this program to taskbar**.

Backstage view

Most ribbon tabs have a set of related tools and commands. The File tab, though, opens Backstage view. This view gives you access to saving and printing, document information and protection, program options, and more.

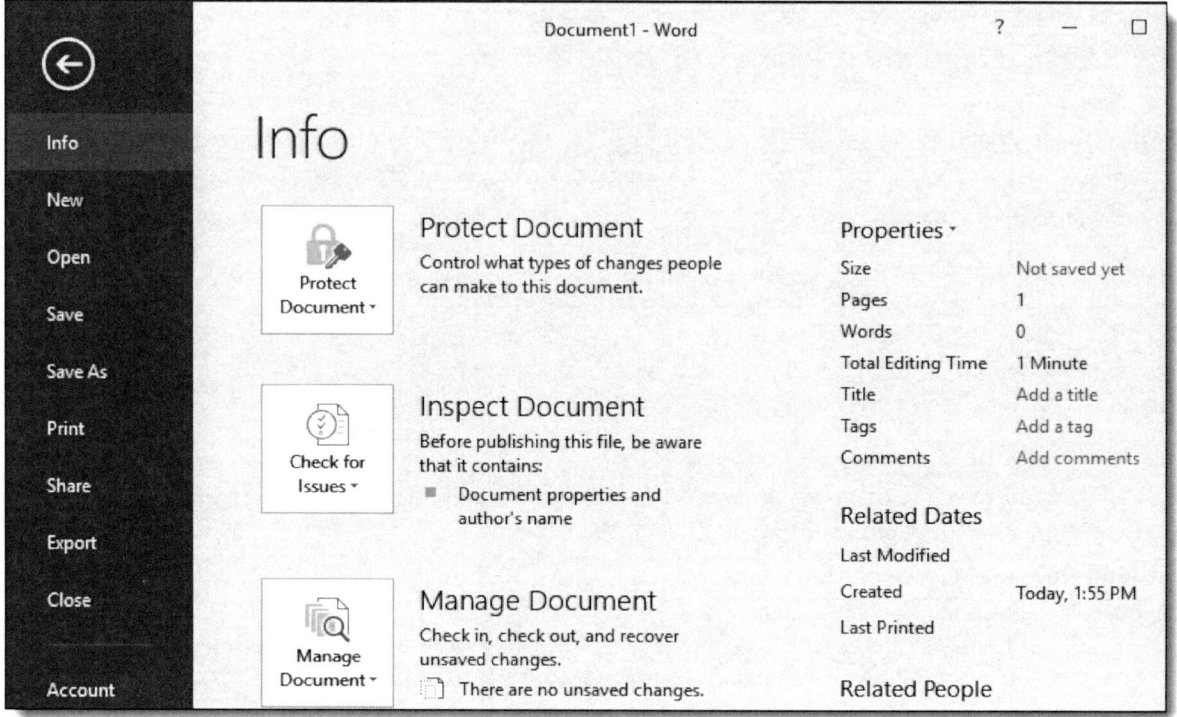

To return to your document, click the arrow at the top left.

Opening a document

When you start Word, a startup screen gives you the choice of opening a recent document, a blank document, an existing document, or one based on a template. Once you've opened a blank document, if you leave it blank and then open another document, the blank document automatically closes without being saved.

 Note: Opening downloaded files in Office applications can result in the document being displayed in Protected view. To be able to make and save changes to a document in Protected view, click **Enable Editing** at the top of the document window.

 Exam Objective: MOS Word Core 1.1.1

1. On the File tab, click **Open**.

    You will see various options for locations on the left, and a list of recently opened documents (if any) on the right.

2. Either click a file to open it, or click a location to display the **Open** window.

3. Navigate to the document you want to open, select it, and click **Open**.

    You can instead double-click the file.

After you've opened documents, they will appear in the Recent section of Backstage view. You can re-open files from there without browsing for them. If you open a document when you already have another document open, it opens in a new window. One exception is if you open a document when you first start Word; in that case, the new document replaces the blank document that opens with Word.

Closing documents

Each document in Word opens in its own window. There are several ways to close documents. If you haven't yet saved the document you're trying to close, you'll be asked if you want to do so.

- On the File tab, click **Close**.

    If more than one document is open, that particular document closes; any other document(s) remains open. If it is the only Word document open, the blank Word window remains open.

- Click the close button ☒ in the upper-right corner.

    If this is the only Word document open, Word closes as well.

- To close one of multiple open documents, right-click the Word taskbar icon, hover over the document, and click its close button.

- To close all open documents, right-click the Word taskbar icon, and click **Close all windows**.

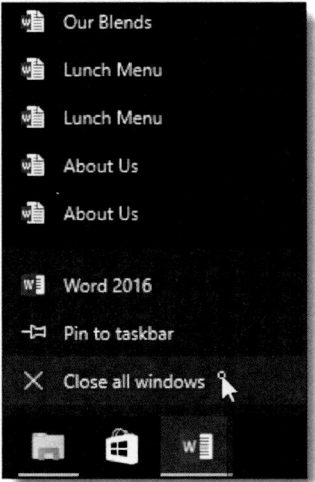

Depending on your graphics settings, you might see thumbnail pictures instead of document names.

Whichever way you choose to close a document, you'll be prompted to save any unsaved changes.

Customizing the Quick Access toolbar

You can easily add commands to or remove them from the Quick Access toolbar to better suit the way you like to work.

 Exam Objective: MOS Word Core 1.4.3

1. Click the Customize Quick Access Toolbar button.
   On the right of the Quick Access toolbar.

   To display the Customize Quick Access Toolbar menu.

   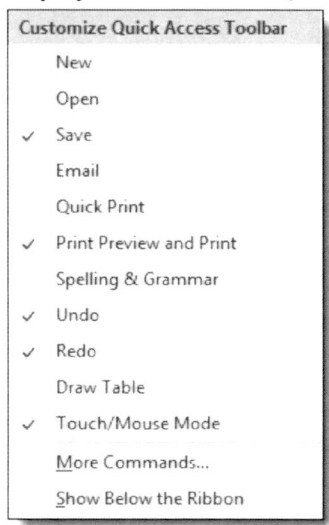

2. Click a command in the menu to show or hide it.
   The commands that are shown on the toolbar will have a checkmark.

3. To add other commands, click **More Commands**.
   The Customize the Quick Access Toolbar screen appears in the **Word Options** window. Here, you can choose any command in Word to add to the Quick Access toolbar.

4. Click **OK** to accept your changes and close the window.

Exercise: Getting around Word

 Exam Objective: MOS Word Core 1.1.1

Do This	How & Why
1. Click **Start > All apps > Word 2016**.	To start Microsoft Word 2016. You will see the startup screen.
2. In the startup screen, click **Blank document**.	The Word window opens to a blank document with the Home tab active. If you see an area on the left of the screen that is called "Navigation," close it by clicking its Close button (the "x").

Do This	How & Why
3. Observe the commands on the Home tab.	These are mostly commands for formatting text and paragraphs. The Clipboard group helps you to move text around.
4. Open the Font window.	
a) In the Font group, in the lower-right, click the Font button.	
	To open the Font window.
b) Observe the font options.	There are many options for formatting text.
c) Click the **Advanced** tab.	These options allow fine control over formatting, such as character spacing.
d) Close the Font window.	Click the **Close** button or click **Cancel**.
5. On the Ribbon's View tab, in the Show group, check **Ruler**.	Click its box to check it.
	To show the ruler, which shows you where margins and tab stops are located for the current paragraph.
6. Click the **File** tab.	To display Backstage view.
7. Open About Us from the current chapter's data folder.	
a) On the File tab, click **Open**.	
b) Under Open, click **Browse** to display the **Open** window.	
c) Navigate to the current chapter's data folder.	Follow your instructor's directions.
d) Select **About Us**, and click **Open**.	To open a document with information about Java Tucana, a fictional chain of cafés.
8. On the File tab, click **Close**.	To close the document. Word remains open, but there is no document open.

Assessment: Getting around

1. Which toolbar holds a few common commands and can be customized? Choose the single best answer.

    - Ribbon
    - Group
    - Quick Access
    - Ruler

2. Which view gives you access to saving and printing, document information and protection, and other options?

    - Outline
    - Backstage
    - Info
    - Options

Module B: Creating documents

Creating a document in Word is as simple as starting the program and beginning to type. Much of what you'll do, besides typing, involves cutting and pasting text, and the very important ability to undo an action.

You will learn how to:

- Create a new blank document
- Cut, copy, and paste text
- Undo actions
- Save a document

Creating a new blank document

When you start Word, the startup screen gives you the options to open a new, blank document. You can also do so after Word is open.

Exam Objective: MOS Word Core 1.1.1

1. On the File tab, click **New**.
2. Click **Blank document**.
    A new, blank document opens in a new Word window.
3. Enter text in the document window by typing.
    There are many ways to enter and manipulate text, and you'll be learning about them shortly.

Entering symbols

Sometimes, you will want to enter text that isn't readily available on the keyboard, such as a foreign character (like the French accent aigu over the e, é) or a copyright symbol (©). Word has a gallery of such symbols.

1. Place the insertion point where you want the symbol.
2. On the Insert tab, in the Symbols group, click **Symbol**.
    The Symbol gallery appears, giving you a choice of common or recently-used symbols.

3. Click the symbol you want to place it at the cursor.
    If the symbol you want is not in the gallery, click More Symbols to open the Symbols window, where you can choose from a large variety of symbols.

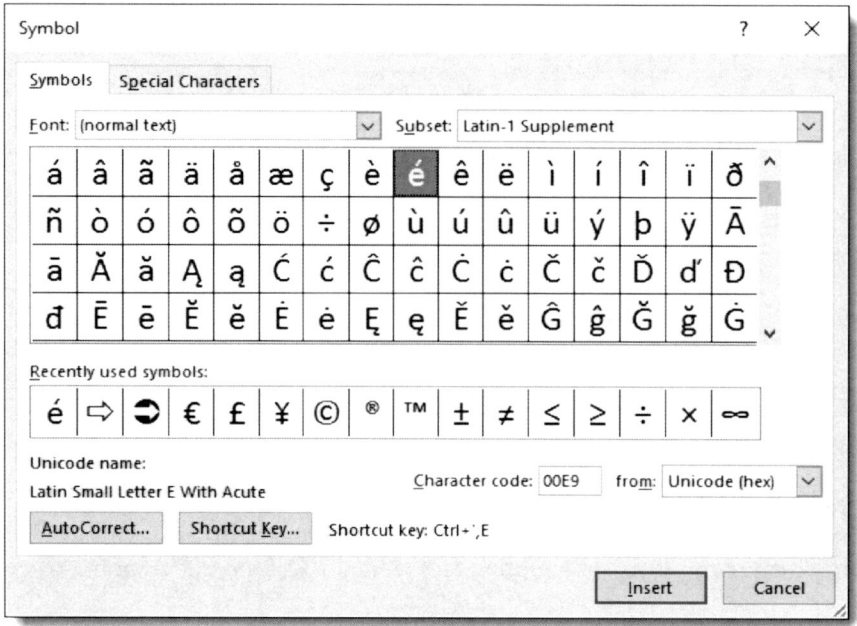

Saving a document

There are several ways to save an open document.

- Click ![save] (the Save button) in the Quick Access toolbar.
- Use the **Ctrl+S** keyboard shortcut.
- On the File tab, click **Save** or **Save As**.
- When you close Word, you're prompted to save any unsaved documents that are open.

Regardless of which method you use, the first time you save a document, you'll see the **Save As** window, which prompts you for a name and location for the file, and offers access to other options. After that, the Save command updates the file with no further prompting.
If you want to change the name or location of a previously saved file, on the File tab, click **Save As > Browse**.

 Note: If saving to a location other than your computer—for example, to OneDrive—you would instead click **OneDrive**.

The Save As window

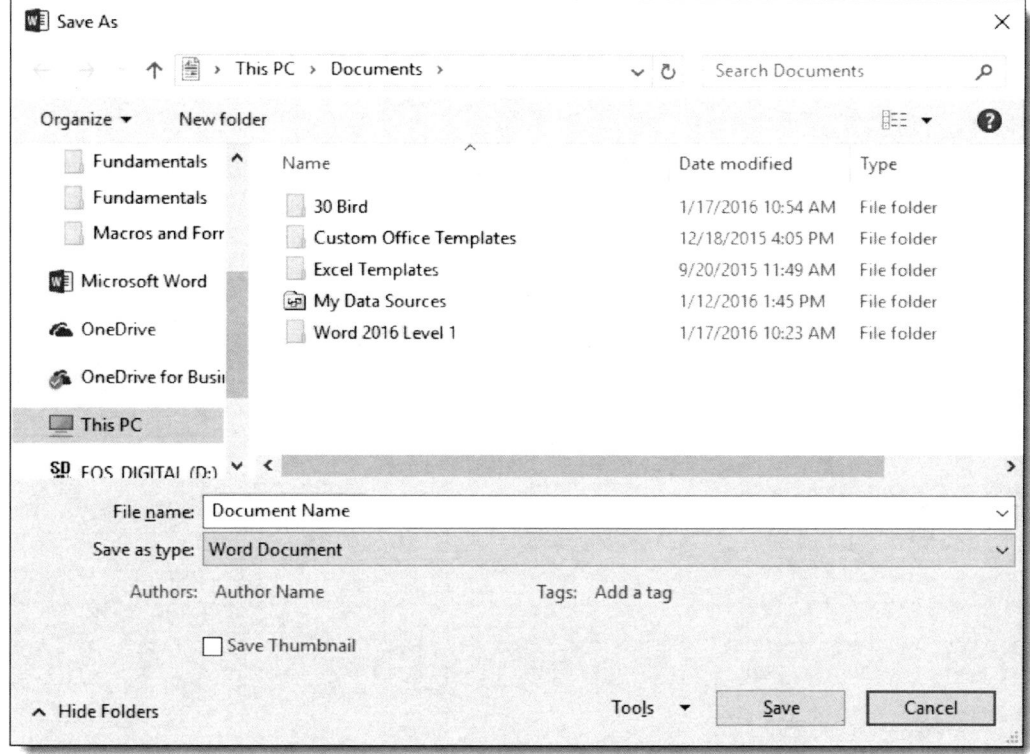

Managing draft versions

If you experience a software crash or a power outage while you're working, there's a chance you won't lose all your work. You might be able to recover some or all of what you were working on, even if you hadn't saved your work. Word keeps temporary copies of open files, and deletes them when you save a document or close it without saving. Unfortunately, this feature does not keep track of previous versions of a document once you save changes or close it without saving.

 Exam Objective: MOS Word Expert 1.1.3

If Word shuts down suddenly, however, the draft version remains on your hard disk. Often, the Document Recovery pane will be open when you restart Word, and you can recover the document from there.

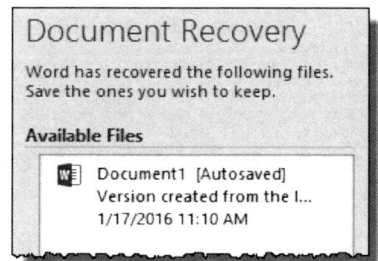

If the Document Recovery pane does not open, or you want to search for earlier unsaved draft versions, you can use the Manage Versions button in Backstage view.

- To recover a draft version, on the File tab, click **Info**, then click **Manage Documents > Recover Unsaved Documents**. Select the document you want, and click **Open**.

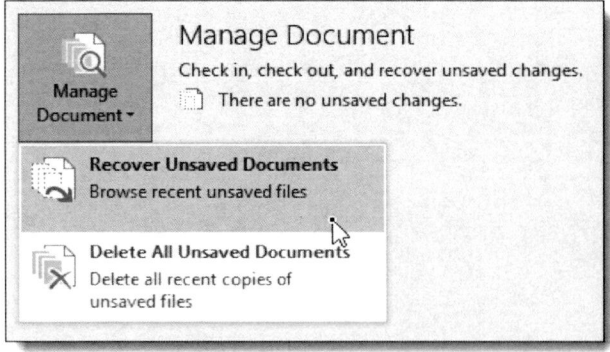

- If you are sure you don't need the unsaved files, click **Manage Documents > Delete All Unsaved Documents**.

Exercise: Creating a new document

Word is open with no documents open.

 Exam Objective: MOS Word Core 1.1.1, 2.1.2

Do This	How & Why
1. Start a new, blank document: a) On the File tab, click **New**. b) Click **Blank document**.	
2. Observe the title bar.	It shows a generic document name. Document1 - Word
3. Enter some of the following information: • Your occupation • Your name • Your address • Your phone number • Your email address	Press **Enter** after each line. If you don't want to use your own information, make up something.
4. Save the document:	The document is saved and you return to the document window.
a) In Backstage view, click **Save**.	"Backstage view" is what you see when you click the File tab. Because this document has never been saved, the **Save As** window opens.
b) Click Browse, then navigate to the current chapter's data folder.	Follow your instructor's directions.
c) In the File name box, type `Contact Info`.	

Do This	How & Why
d) Click **Save**.	
5. Observe the title bar.	It shows the file name you entered.
6. Change the occupation text.	
a) Drag over the text.	*Editor* *Johnny Lightning* To select it. You will briefly see a gallery of formatting options when you select the text. You'll learn about that soon. For now, move the mouse slightly and the gallery will disappear.
b) Type a different occupation.	The text you type replaces the selected text. If you had just placed the cursor somewhere, what you typed would have been inserted.
7. Click 🖫 .	On the Quick Access toolbar. You can also you the keyboard shortcut, **Ctrl+S**. To save your change to the document. When you click the Save button, the file is saved in the same location and with the same name. To change the name or location, you would click Save As in Backstage view.
8. At the end of the document, press **Enter** to create a new paragraph.	You will enter a symbol here. Not all of the text you will need is readily available on the keyboard.
9. On the Insert tab, click Symbol.	To display the symbol gallery. Common and recently-used symbols appear here. As you work more with Word, you'll almost always find the symbols you use most here.
10. Click ©.	To insert the copyright symbol in the document. If you don't see the copyright symbol, try another.
11. Click **Symbol**, then click **More Symbols**.	To display the Symbol window. Here, you can choose from a huge variety of symbols in many fonts.
12. Click **Cancel**.	
13. Close the document.	Try clicking the Close box on the far right of the title bar. Word prompts you to save your changes. When you attempt to close a document without having saved your most recent changes, you will see this.
14. Click **Don't Save**.	To close the document without saving changes.

Manipulating text

The most basic way to get information into your documents is to type it. But you will also want to move text after entering it, or copy it to a second location. In order to do that, you'll need to know how to select text (which is also important for formatting). There are many techniques for moving and copying text, and a great variety of selection techniques that use the mouse, the keyboard, or both. You should familiarize yourself with as many of these techniques as possible in order to be an efficient, productive user of Word.

Moving the cursor

Selecting text

There are many ways to select text so that you can then format, copy, or delete it.

- Double-click a word to select it.
- Triple-click in a paragraph to select it.
- Drag over text to select multiple words or paragraphs.
- Hold down Shift and use the arrow keys to extend the selection from the current cursor position. You can also use the **Home**, **End**, **Page Up**, and **Page Down** keys.
- Click or drag in the left margin to select lines.
- Press **Ctrl+A** to select all text in a document.

Exercise: Moving the cursor and selecting text

Do This	How & Why
1. Open About Us and save it as About Us Selecting.	You'll use this document to experiment with techniques for moving the cursor and selecting text.
2. Use the arrow keys to move the cursor.	The most basic keyboard technique for moving the cursor (or the "insertion point") is to press the arrow keys. Left and right move one character at a time, up and down one line at a time. This is efficient when you're moving to a location that is close to the current location.
3. Press **Ctrl+Home**.	This will always bring you to the top of the document.
4. While holding **Ctrl**, press the right arrow key a few times.	Each time will move the cursor one word to the right. Holding Ctrl while pressing left arrow, similarly, moves one word to the left. Ctrl plus the up or down arrow keys moves the cursor a paragraph at a time.
5. Place the cursor in the first full paragraph, then press **End**.	To move to the end of the current line.
6. What does pressing **Home** do?	By itself, pressing **Home** takes you to the beginning of the current line. You've already seen that pressing **Ctrl+Home** will take you to the beginning of the document. **Ctrl+End** move to the end of the document.

Do This	How & Why
7. Click at the beginning of the document.	To move the cursor there. You can always place the cursor by clicking where you want it.
8. Drag over "About Java Tucana".	To select it. You can always select text by dragging.
9. Chile holding **Shift**, click at the end of the first full paragraph.	To extend the selection to include everything from the current selection through the point at which you clicked. This can be useful for selecting larger areas of text.
10. Try using **Shift** with the other selection techniques.	Shift with an arrow key extends the selection by one character or one line. Using Ctrl+Shift with an arrow key extends the selection one word or one paragraph at a time. You should practice these techniques and become familiar with them. Staying on the keyboard can really increase your productivity.
11. Double-click a word.	To select it.
12. Triple-click within a paragraph.	To select the entire paragraph. This can be very handy. As you can see, there are many ways to select text and to move the cursor. You should try a variety of techniques to see which work best for you in different situations.

Cutting and copying text

Deleting text removes the text without saving it. Cutting text removes the text but keeps a copy of it in a special location called *the clipboard* for further use. Copying text leaves the text in place *and* saves a copy to the clipboard. After you've placed text on the clipboard, you can use Paste commands to put it elsewhere.

Exam Objective: MOS Word Core 2.1.2

- To delete selected text, press **Delete** or **Backspace** on the keyboard.
  Pressing either of these keys with no text selected will delete one character at a time at the location of the cursor: **Delete** removes the character immediately to the *right*; **Backspace** deletes the character immediately to the *left*.

- There are three ways to cut selected text:
  - Press **Ctrl+X** on the keyboard.
  - Right-click the selected text, and click **Cut**.
  - On the Home tab, click ✂ Cut .

- Similarly, there are three ways to copy selected text:
  - Press **Ctrl+C** on the keyboard.
  - Right-click the selected text, and click **Copy**.
  - On the Home tab, click 📋 Copy .

Pasting text

There are several methods and options for pasting text from the clipboard.

 Exam Objective: MOS Word Core 2.1.2

- Right-click where you want to paste, and click one of these paste options:
    - **Keep source formatting**: Pastes clipboard contents with only its original formatting intact.
    - **Merge formatting**: Pasted contents are applied with a blend of original and destination formats.
    - **Keep text only** (adopt destination formatting): Retains the original text but with destination formats applied.
- On the Home tab, click **Paste**.
    This uses the current default paste options. Click the drop-down arrow under the button for more options.

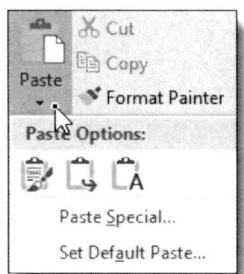

- Press **Ctrl+V** on the keyboard.
    This uses the current default paste option.
- Another way to cut and paste in one move is to drag selected text to its new location.

Using Undo

You can undo almost any number of actions while you have a document open. However, once you close and reopen a document, the Undo stack for that document is cleared. There are two common ways to undo actions.

- Press **Ctrl+Z**.
    To undo the most recent action. Hold down **Ctrl** and press **Z** multiple times to step back through and undo multiple actions.
- Click (the Undo button).
    To undo the most recent action. Click it multiple times to step back through actions. You can also use the drop-down list to select an action. All actions since the one you've selected are undone.

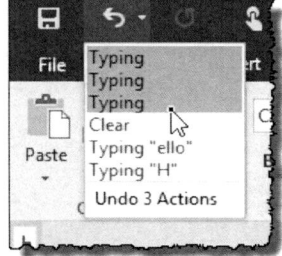

Exercise: Moving and copying text

About Us Selecting should be open at the beginning of this exercise.

Do This	How & Why
1. Move the Java Tucana Coffee and Tea section above the Java Tucana Services section.	
a) Select the entire Java Tucana Coffee and Tea section.	You can drag over it, or try another method, such as clicking at the beginning of the heading, then Shift-clicking at the end of the document.
b) Click **Cut**.	In the Clipboard group on the left of the Home tab. To remove the selected text from the document and place it in a temporary location called the clipboard.
c) Click before the Java Tucana Services heading.	Here.
d) Click **Paste**.	The Paste button is the Clipboard group on the Home tab.
	The cut text now appears before the other text. Moving text like this is a four step process: select the text to move, cut it, select the location to paste it, then paste it. There are faster ways, though, in many situations.
2. Undo the paste.	Click the Undo button on the Quick Access toolbar.
3. Click again.	To undo the cut. The undo button keeps track of many of your last actions. You'll now use a different method to move the text.
4. Move the text by using the mouse.	
a) Select the entire Java Tucana Coffee and Tea section.	
Continued...	

Do This	How & Why
b) Drag the selected text before the Java Tucana Coffee and Tea heading.	As you drag, there is a box attached to the pointer, and the insertion point shows where the text will appear.
5. Save the document.	Click the Save button on the Quick Access toolbar.
6. Copy the heading "Java Tucana's Blends" and the list of blends.	
a) Select the paragraphs.	
b) Press **Ctrl+C**.	To copy the selection to the clipboard. Notice that the selected text is not removed when you copy it (unlike when you cut it). You could also have clicked the Copy button in the Clipboard group of the home tab.
c) Place the cursor at the beginning of the Java Tucana Services heading.	You will paste the copied text here.
d) Press **Ctrl+V**.	To paste the text here. You could also have clicked the Paste button.
7. Edit the text as shown.	You'll need to delete the teas from the first list, edit the second heading, and delete the two coffee blends from the second list.
8. Save the document.	Click the Save button, or press **Ctrl+S**.
9. Do you know how to copy text using the mouse?	You can do this by holding down **Ctrl** while dragging selected text. If your instructor says you have time, experiment with copying using the mouse.
10. Close the document.	You do not need to save any changes.

Assessment: Creating documents

1. If you click Save in a document you haven't saved before, the Save As window opens instead. True or false?

    - True.
    - False.

2. What is the keyboard shortcut for selecting everything in a document?

    - Ctrl+A
    - Ctrl+E
    - Ctrl+S
    - Alt+E

3. What is the keyboard shortcut to paste text?

    - Ctrl+P
    - Alt+P
    - Alt+V
    - Ctrl+V

Module C: Document views

Word offers several ways to view a document, and the ability to zoom in and out. You can also switch between multiple documents or view them side by side.

You will learn:

- About different document views
- How to split a document window
- How to view and switch between multiple open documents
- How to use Zoom features

Document views

There are five document views. You select which to use, either on the status bar or on the View tab.

 Exam Objective: MOS Word Core 1.4.1

Document views on the View tab

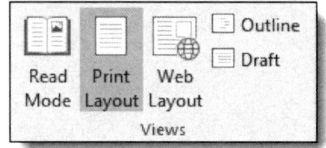

Read Mode   Maximizes area for reading and commenting. Provides tools to research, translate, highlight, and comment.

Print Layout   Shows how the document will look printed on the page.

Web Layout   Shows what the document will look like saved as a web page.

Outline   Shows the document in outline form and provides outline tools.

Draft   Used mainly for editing content. Headers, footers, and print layout are not visible.

Besides different document views, Word allows you to split the document window, to view two documents side by side, to switch between any number of open documents, and to zoom in and out while viewing a document.

Splitting a document window

You can split the document window so you can see and edit different parts of the same document.

 Exam Objective: MOS Word Core 1.4.4

1. On the View tab, in the Window group, click **Split**.

   The document window splits into two windows, each with its own scroll bars. You can edit in either window. The Split command changes to "Remove Split."

2. To resize the windows, drag the dividing bar up or down.

3. To remove the split: on the View tab, in the Windows Group, click **Remove Split**; or just double-click the bar dividing the windows.

Viewing documents side by side

You can view two documents side by side, and if you want, synchronize scrolling between them. You need to have at least two documents open to use this feature.

1. On the View tab, in the Window group, click **View Side by Side**.
2. If more than two documents are open, select the other document you want to view, and click **OK**.
    The two documents appear side by side, taking up the whole screen. By default, synchronized scrolling is enabled. That is, when you scroll in one window, the other scrolls also.
3. To toggle synchronized scrolling, on the View tab, click the **Synchronized Scrolling** button.
4. If the windows get moved or misaligned, click **Reset Window Position** to return them to full-screen, side-by-side view.

Switching between open documents

If you have more than one Word document open, there are at least four ways you can switch between them.

- Click any part of the window to which you want to switch, if it's visible.
- Click or hover over the Word icon on the taskbar. When a list of open documents appears, click the document you want.
    Depending on the graphics options you've set, this is either a list of document titles or thumbnails of each window, with titles.
- Hold down **Alt** and press **Tab** repeatedly until you select the document you want, then release **Alt**.
    Doing so flips through all open programs, not just Word documents. Exactly what this looks like varies, depending on your graphics settings.

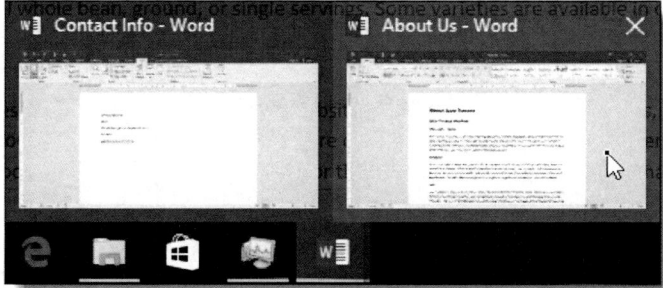

- On the View tab, in the Window group, click **Switch Windows**, and select the document you'd like.

Selecting Zoom options

There are three options for using the Zoom feature.

Exam Objective: MOS Word Core 1.4.2

- Press and hold down the **Ctrl** key, and roll the mouse wheel forward or backward to zoom in and out, effectively enlarging and reducing the document elements, respectively.
- Use the Zoom control at the right end of the status bar. Click the plus or minus buttons, or drag the slider.

- Use the commands in the Zoom group on the View tab.

Exercise: Changing document views

Exam Objective: MOS Word Core 1.4.1, 1.4.2, 1.4.4

Do This	How & Why
1. Open the documents `About Us`, `Our Services`, and `Our Blends`.	From the `Fundamentals` folder. **Note:** Opening downloaded files in Office applications can result in the documents being displayed in Protected view. This can be overridden by clicking **Enable Editing** at the top of the document window.
2. Observe the Word icon in the taskbar.	It shows several documents open.
3. Point to the Word icon.	Depending on your graphics settings, you'll see a list of file names or thumbnail images of open files.
4. Click one of the open files.	One that isn't currently active in Word. To switch to that file.
5. Switch to `About Us`.	If necessary.
6. On the View tab, click **Split**.	To split the window. You can now scroll separately in each window, viewing different parts of the same document at the same time.
7. Remove the split using one of these methods: • On the View tab, click **Remove Split**. • Double-click the split line.	
8. Try different Zoom features: • Hold down the **Ctrl** key, and scroll the mouse wheel. • On the right of the status bar, use the slider. • On the View tab, use the Zoom group options.	

Do This	How & Why
9. On the View tab, in the Zoom group, click **100%**.	
10. On the View tab, click **View Side by Side**.	
11. Select one of the other documents, and click **OK**.	The documents each take up half of the screen.
12. Try scrolling in one of the documents.	Notice that both documents scroll. By default, when you view documents side-by-side, their scrolling is synchronized. You can turn this off by clicking the Synchronous Scrolling option on the View tab.
13. Close all open documents.	
14. Close Word.	

Assessment: Document views

1. If you click View Side by Side with more than two documents open, what happens?

    - You have to choose which other document to view.
    - Documents are arranged in columns.
    - Nothing happens.
    - You can't; the option is grayed out.

2. Which of these actions will cause the document to zoom in?

    - Ctrl+I
    - Alt+Z
    - Ctrl+Up Arrow
    - Ctrl+Mouse wheel forward

Summary: Fundamentals

You should now know:

- About the Word interface, Backstage view, and opening and closing documents
- How to create blank documents; save, cut, and paste text; and undo actions
- How to change the view of a document, split the document window, view documents side by side, zoom in and out, and switch between open documents

Synthesis: Fundamentals

In this synthesis exercise, you'll start Word, open two documents, and experiment with various view options.

1. Start Word.
2. Open `Lunch Menu` and `About Us`.
   From the `Fundamentals` folder.
3. View the documents side by side.
4. Split the document window in the About Us document.
5. Zoom in and out on the menu.
   Try different methods: keyboard, status bar, and Zoom group.
6. Save `Lunch Menu` as `Lunch Menu Edited`.
7. In the menu, make the Surf and Surf item first under the Lunch Menu heading.
8. Save the menu and then close it.
9. Try different document views for About Us.
10. Close the document.
    Leave Word open.

Chapter 2: Formatting

You will learn:

- How to format characters
- How to format paragraphs
- About Quick Styles, style sets, and themes
- How to create bulleted and numbered lists

Module A: Formatting characters

It's important to understand the difference between character and paragraph attributes. You can avoid some confusion and frustration by knowing when and how to apply each. The simplest type of formatting is character formatting, things like making a word bold or italic, increasing its size, or changing its font.

You will learn:

- How to format characters
- How to use Format Painter

Formatting characters

Word allows you to change many visual attributes of the text. Most of these attributes you might never need to change. There are a few attributes, though, that you'll probably adjust quite often.

Font Also called font face or typeface, this is the actual shape of the characters. Examples include Arial, Helvetica, and Times New Roman.

Font size The height, in points, of the largest capital characters. Width is adjusted accordingly. Microsoft Office applications use the American-British point system, which defines a point as 1/72 of an inch (.351 mm).

Font style The term *style* is used in different ways in Word. In this case, it refers the whether or not the font is bold, italic, underline, or any combination of these.

Font color You can choose from many defined colors, or make a color by entering specific color and brightness values. Plus, you can adjust underline and highlight color independently of font color.

Effects These include strikethrough, superscript, and subscript. Not to be confused with *text effects*, which are graphic effects such as 3-D and drop shadows.

Applying character attributes

After you select the text you want to format, there are a number of ways to apply individual character attributes.

 Exam Objective: MOS Word Core 2.2.1, 2.2.5

- Use the commands on the Home tab, in the Font group. Hover the mouse pointer over a command to see its description.

    You can apply many attributes, such as text effects, text highlight color, and font color.

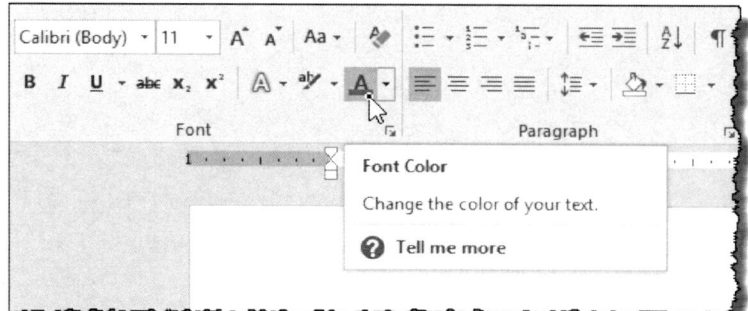

- Click the expansion arrow in the lower-right corner of the Font group to open the **Font** window.
- Right-click selected text, and click **Font** from the shortcut menu.
- Right-click selected text, and use the mini toolbar that appears above the selection.

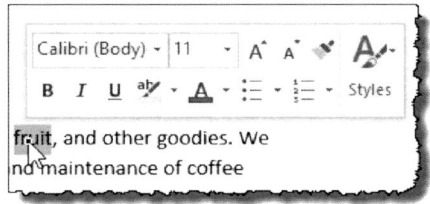

- Use keyboard shortcuts for font styles: **Crtl+B** for bold, **Ctrl+I** for italic, and **Ctrl+U** for underline.

Using Format Painter

You can use Format Painter to copy text formatting from one place and apply it to text in another.

 Exam Objective: MOS Word Core 2.2.2

1. Select the text with the formatting you want to copy.
   If you want to copy the paragraph style as well, select the entire paragraph, including the paragraph mark at the end.
2. On the Home tab, in the Clipboard group, click **Format Painter**.
   To format multiple items, double-click **Format Painter**. This keeps it active for multiple selections.
   The mouse pointer shows a paintbrush when it is over text.
3. Drag the pointer over text you want to format.
   If you are formatting one item, the text is formatted and the pointer returns to normal.
4. If you are formatting multiple items, once you're finished, press **Esc** or click **Format Painter** again to stop formatting.

You can also use format painter to copy some graphic formatting, such as the border, fill color, and 3-D format of a shape.

Exercise: Formatting characters

 Exam Objective: MOS Word Core 2.2.1, 2.2.2, 2.2.5

Do This	How & Why
1. Open `Coffee-text`. Save it as `Coffee-text-formatted`.	The document is in the current chapter's folder, and you should save it there as well.
2. Select the first line.	The heading Java Tucana Coffee.
3. On the Home tab, in the Font group, select **Arial**.	Click the drop-down arrow next to the Font box.
4. From the Font Size list, select **16**.	
5. Press **Ctrl+B**, and then press **Ctrl+I**.	To make the heading bold and italic. You could also use the Bold and Italic buttons in the Font group.
Continued...	

Do This	How & Why
6. Highlight the text "Tucana Roast," in the second full paragraph. a) Select the text. b) In the mini toolbar, click the Text Highlight Color arrow, then click a color you like.	The highlighting appears over the text.
7. Select the "Java Tucana Coffee" heading.	You'll copy it's formatting to another heading.
8. In the Clipboard group, click the **Format Painter** button.	The pointer changes to a paintbrush when it is over text.
9. Select the heading Our Blends.	It takes on the formatting of the first heading, and the pointer returns to normal.
10. In the first paragraph under Our Blends, italicize "Bourbon Santos."	Select it and click $\boxed{I}$.
11. Double-click **Format Painter**.	Be sure that "Bourbon Santos" is still selected. Double-clicking enables Format Painter to be used for multiple selections.
12. In the same paragraph, select "Coban." In the next paragraph, select "Bogota," and then select "Tarrazu."	Note that you can select a whole word by double-clicking it. These are all now italic.
13. Press **Esc**.	To deactivate Format Painter.
14. Save and then close the document.	

The document with formatted text

Java Tucana Coffee

Coffee has been cultivated in South America since the 1700's. Most of the plants are of the Arabica variety, but regional differences in climate, elevation, and soil mean a wide range of flavor, body, and acidity. Java Tucana carries the best South American coffees our buyers can find. We also produce our own blends of coffee.

Our Blends

Tucana Roast, our signature blend, combines Brazilian *Bourbon Santos* with Guatemalan *Coban*. The result is a coffee that is remarkably rich and fragrant yet clean, sweet, and snappy. It's the perfect cup for after a meal or as an afternoon refresher.

Phoenix Roast can help you rise from the ashes of a late night or a long meeting. A blend of Columbian *Bogota* and Costa Rican *Tarrazu*, this cup is full-bodied, fragrant, and complex, but never bitter. Its rich flavor and clean finish make it the perfect coffee for the first cup of the day.

Assessment: Formatting characters

1. Helvetica and Arial are examples of what? Choose the single best answer.

    - Font size
    - Font face
    - Font effects
    - Font style

2. Which of the following are examples of character formatting? Select all correct answers.

    - Font size
    - Line spacing
    - Alignment
    - Font style

Module B: Formatting paragraphs

Paragraph formatting applies to everything in a paragraph: where it appears on the page, its alignment, indents, tabs, spacing, and much more.

You will learn how to:

- Apply paragraph attributes such as alignment and spacing
- Control indenting for paragraphs
- Control tab settings for paragraphs

Paragraph attributes

In Word, a paragraph is any number of words, even just one (or none at all), ending with (or consisting of) a paragraph mark. To see the paragraph mark and other hidden characters, click the **Show/Hide** button on the Home tab in the Paragraph group.

You can consider the paragraph's attributes to be attached to its paragraph mark. The attributes most commonly changed are alignment, indentation, and spacing.

Alignment	The paragraph can be justified right, center, left, or full.
Outline level	The level of the paragraph in a bulleted or numbered list.
Indentation	You can indent the left and/or right edge of the paragraph. You can also indent the first line only, or create a hanging indent (all lines except the first).
Spacing	Spacing before and after a paragraph, as well as the line spacing within it.
Color and border	You can put a line border around a paragraph and change its background color. If the color is dark, the text color is automatically white in contrast to it.

Applying paragraph attributes

To change attributes of several paragraphs, they should be selected, including the paragraph mark at the end of the selection. To change the attributes of a single paragraph, though, the cursor just needs to be placed anywhere in the paragraph; the entire paragraph does not have to be selected.

 Exam Objective: MOS Word Core 2.2.3

- Use the options available on the Home tab, in the Paragraph group.
    Hover the pointer over a command to see its description.

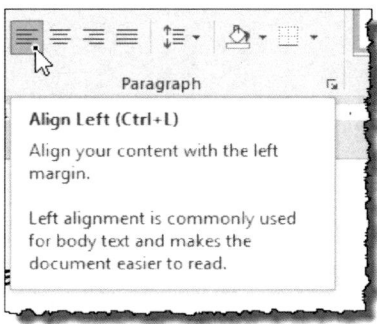

- To open the **Paragraph** window, click the Paragraph Settings button in the lower-right of the Paragraph ribbon group.

    You can instead right-click the selected paragraph(s) and click **Paragraph**.

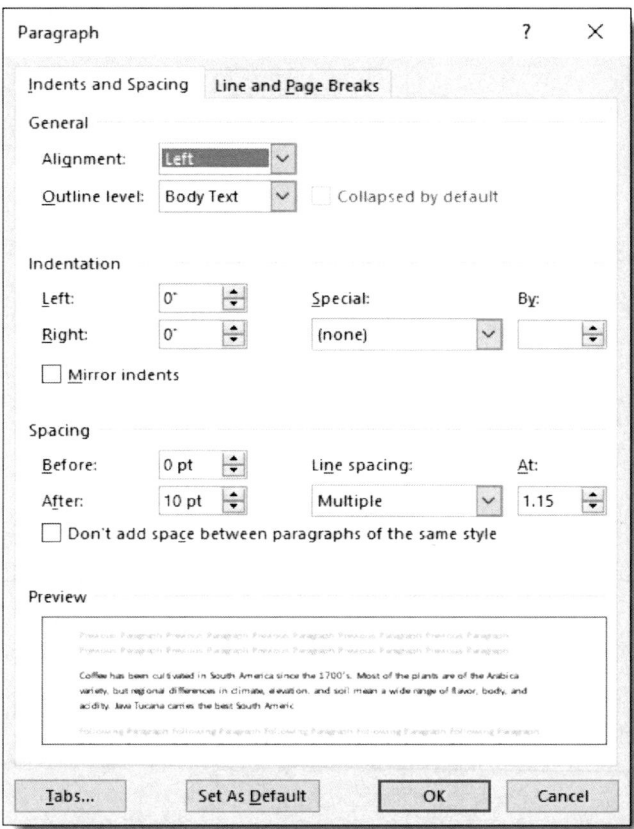

- Indents and tabs can also be set by clicking and dragging markers directly on the ruler. Hover the mouse pointer over a marker to see its description.

Setting line spacing

You can change the spacing before and after paragraphs and between lines in a paragraph.

After you select the paragraphs you want to format, either use the **Line and Paragraph Spacing** button, or open the **Paragraph** window.

1. On the Home tab, in the Paragraph group, click the **Line and Paragraph Spacing** button, and select an option.

   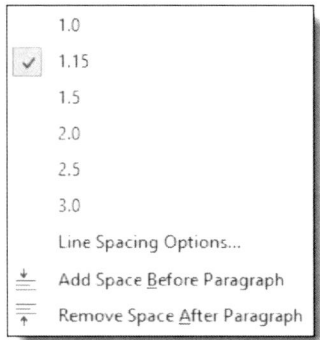

2. If you need more spacing options, click **Line Spacing Options**.
   To open the **Paragraph** window, which you can also do from the lower-right corner of the Paragraph group.

   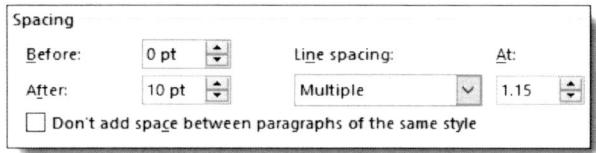

3. Set the spacing options, and click **OK**.
   The Add Space Before Paragraph and Add Space After Paragraph options set spacing above and below entire paragraphs, respectively. You can also choose not to add space between paragraphs of the same style.

Exercise: Controlling alignment and spacing

Exam Objective: MOS Word Core 2.2.3

Do This	How & Why
1. Open `Coffee-paragraphs` and save it as `Coffee-paragraphs-formatted`.	This is similar to the document you applied character formatting to.
2. Place the cursor in the first full paragraph.	Click anywhere in the paragraph beginning, "Coffee has been cultivated..."

Do This	How & Why
3. In the Paragraph Group, click [icon].	To display the Line and Paragraph Spacing menu. Here, you change the space between paragraphs, or choose commands to open the Paragraph window where you will have finer control. [Line and Paragraph Spacing menu showing: 1.0, 1.15 (checked), 1.5, 2.0, 2.5, 3.0, Line Spacing Options..., Add Space Before Paragraph, Remove Space After Paragraph]
4. Click **1.5**.	To change the space between lines of the current paragraph to 1.5 lines. When you change line spacing, it applies to all lines in the selected paragraph.
5. In the Paragraph group, observe the alignment buttons.	The Align Left button is highlighted, because the paragraph is aligned along the left margin (as paragraphs are by default).
6. Click [icon].	To center-align the paragraph.
7. Right-align the paragraph.	Click [icon]. Alignment along the right margin is unusual but sometimes useful.
8. Justify the paragraph.	Click [icon]. This is how we want the paragraph, with both margins aligned, like in a newspaper.
9. Apply the same formatting to the other two descriptive paragraphs.	
a) Double-click **Format Painter**.	
b) Click once in each of the other paragraphs.	There's no need to select them.
c) Press **Esc**.	To turn off the Format Painter.
10. Update the document and compare it to the results below.	

After you've completed the exercise, the document should look like the following figure:

> ### *Java Tucana Coffee*
>
> Coffee has been cultivated in South America since the 1700's. Most of the plants are of the Arabica variety, but regional differences in climate, elevation, and soil mean a wide range of flavor, body, and acidity. Java Tucana carries the best South American coffees our buyers can find. We also produce our own blends of coffee.
>
> ### *Our Blends*
>
> Tucana Roast, our signature blend, combines Brazilian *Bourbon Santos* with Guatemalan *Coban*. The result is a coffee that is remarkably rich and fragrant yet clean, sweet, and snappy. It's the perfect cup for after a meal or as an afternoon refresher.
>
> Phoenix Roast can help you rise from the ashes of a late night or a long meeting. A blend of Colombian *Bogota* and Costa Rican *Tarrazu*, this cup is full-bodied, fragrant, and complex, but never bitter. Its rich flavor and clean finish make it the perfect coffee for the first cup of the day.

Setting indents

You can apply an indent or hanging indent to the first line of a paragraph, or indent the entire left and/or right edge of the paragraph.

After you select the paragraphs you want to format, there are two places to set indents: the ruler and the Paragraph window. The latter provides more precision.

- On the ruler, drag the First Line Indent, Left Indent, and Right Indent markers to where you want them on the ruler. Hover the mouse pointer over the marker to see its description.

- On the Home tab, in the Paragraph group, open the **Paragraph** window. Set the options in the Indentation sections. The Special drop-down list provides options for first line and hanging indents. When you are done, click **OK**.

    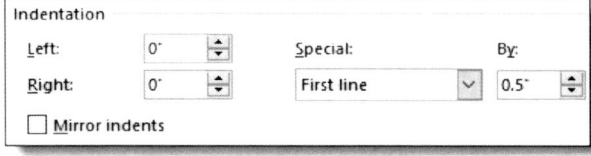

Exercise: Controlling indentation of paragraphs

Coffee-paragraphs-formatted should be open.

 Exam Objective: MOS Word Core 2.2.3

Do This	How & Why
1. Click within the first full paragraph.	The one that begins "Coffee has been cultivated...". You will change experiment with the indenting of the paragraph.

Do This	How & Why
2. On the ruler, drag the Left Indent box to the half-inch mark.	The Left Indent box is the bottom, square one of the three indent icons. 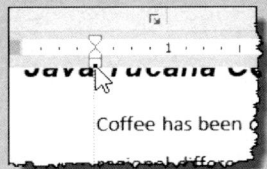
3. Point to each of the triangular indent icons.	To view their screen tips. The top triangle is the First Line Indent marker. Use this to control where the first line of a paragraph begins. The right triangle is the Hanging Indent marker, which controls where all the lines after the first begin. 
4. Drag the Hanging Indent icon back to the zero mark.	To make all the lines after the first align with the left margin. The paragraph should look like this. Notice that the First Line Indent icon is at the half-inch mark on the ruler. 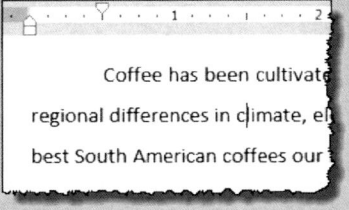
5. With the cursor in the same paragraph, click the Paragraph Settings button.	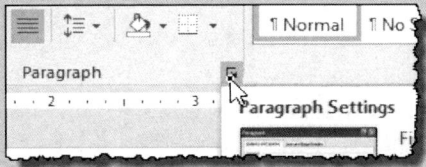 To open the Paragraph window to the Indents and Spacing tab.
6. Observe the Indentation settings.	They reflect the indents you set on the ruler. There is no left or right indent, but the first line is .5 inches to the right.
7. Set left and right indents for the paragraph at 0.5 inches.	Change the values in the Left and Right boxes to 0.5, then click **OK**. The paragraph is indented a half inch from both sides. 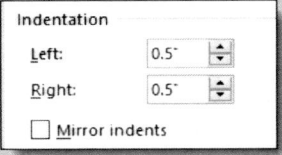
8. Copy the formatting of the paragraph to the other two under "Our Blends".	Select the paragraph, click the Format Painter, and then drag over the other two paragraphs.
9. Save and then close the document.	An example follows.

The document with indented paragraphs

Java Tucana Coffee

Coffee has been cultivated in South America since the 1700's. Most of the plants are of the Arabica variety, but regional differences in climate, elevation, and soil mean a wide range of flavor, body, and acidity. Java Tucana carries the best South American coffees our buyers can find. We also produce our own blends of coffee.

Our Blends

Tucana Roast, our signature blend, combines Brazilian Bourbon Santos with Guatemalan Coban. The result is a coffee that is remarkably rich and fragrant yet clean, sweet, and snappy. It's the perfect cup for after a meal or as an afternoon refresher.

Phoenix Roast can help you rise from the ashes of a late night or a long meeting. A blend of Colombian Bogota and Costa Rican Tarrazu, this cup is full-bodied, fragrant, and complex, but never bitter. Its rich flavor and clean finish make it the perfect coffee for the first cup of the day.

Tabs

Tab stops are the locations to which the cursor skips when you press the **Tab** key on your keyboard. To see tab stops in a document, the ruler has to be showing. If necessary, check **Ruler** in the Show group on the View tab.

Ruler with custom tab stops

By default, there are tab stops every half inch. You can change the distance between default tabs. You can also add custom tab stops with different alignments and leaders. These will appear as bold marks directly on the ruler, with different marks for different types of tab stops.

Tab stops can be set and cleared using the ruler or the **Tabs** window. The latter provides better precision and more options. When you set a custom tab stop, the default tab stops to the left of it are cleared.

Note that added tab stops are paragraph attributes, and they behave like other paragraph attributes. For instance, if you create new tab stops and then press Enter, the new paragraph will inherit the same stops. However, if you create tab stops in one paragraph and then move to a different existing paragraph, those stops will no longer apply. To add tab stops to multiple existing paragraphs, you need to select them all first.

Tab stop types

Whether you set tab stops from the ruler or in the **Tabs** window, you have five types to choose from.

Tab types in Word

Ruler icon	Name	Description
L	Left tab	Text is left-aligned to the stop.
⊥	Center tab	Text is center-aligned to the stop.
⌐	Right tab	Text is right-aligned to the stop.
⊥.	Decimal tab	The decimal point is aligned to the stop. Usually used for a column of numbers.
I	Bar tab	Draws a vertical bar at the stop position. Text entered at this tab stop is left-aligned.

Setting tabs on the ruler

The simplest way to add tab stops is to use the ruler. If the ruler isn't showing, you need to click the **View Ruler** button in the upper-right corner of the document window.

1. Select the paragraph(s) to which you want to apply tab stops.
2. To the left of the top ruler, click the tab icon.
   Multiple times, if necessary, to step through the tab types. Note that you also step through indent icons.

3. Click the ruler where you want the tab stops.
   New tab markers are added to the ruler. The default tab stops are cleared from the left margin up to your custom tab stops.
4. To move a stop you've already set, drag it left or right.

Exercise: Understanding types of tab stops

Do This	How & Why
1. Open Coffee-tabs and save it as Coffee-tabs-formatted.	This document contains information about Java Tucana's coffees. You will format the lists of information using tab stops and tabs.
2. Click ¶ .	To show paragraph and other symbols in the document. When working with tabs, it's often useful to show symbols. These symbols will not print, but can help you to better control formatting.
3. Select all the paragraphs under "Coffees by Region".	When setting tab stops, it's very important to first select all the paragraphs to which you want to apply the same settings. If you do them one at a time, you will almost certainly get inconsistent results.
4. Observe the left tab icon.	It looks like the letter "L". By clicking the ruler, you will create a left-aligned tab stop.
5. Click at the 2-inch mark on the ruler.	To place a left tab stop for the selected paragraphs. But the text doesn't move. Creating tabs is a two-step process: you must set the tab stops and enter tab characters. The order in which you do these two steps doesn't actually matter.
6. Click right before the word "Region" and press **Tab**.	To insert a tab character between "Type" and "Region", which will act as the headings for the rest of the information. The word is now left-aligned at the two-inch mark on the ruler. Note that with symbols showing, you can see the tab character.

Do This	How & Why
7. Insert the rest of the tab characters as shown.	Type· → Region¶ Bogota·Supremo· → Colombia¶ Tarrazu· → Costa·Rica¶ Guatemalan· → Coban¶ Andes·Organic· → Peru¶ Phoenix·Roast· → Africa/Indonesia¶ Tucana·Roast· → South·America¶
8. Replace the left tab stop with a right tab stop.	
a) Select all the paragraphs containing tabs.	
b) Drag the left tab stop off the ruler.	
c) Click the tab icon twice to activate the Right Tab icon.	Right Tab
d) Click at the 2-inch mark on the ruler.	Because the tab characters are already in the paragraphs, you immediately see the result. Placing a right-aligned tab stop at 2 inches makes the text kind of crowded. Andes·Organic· → Peru¶ Phoenix·Roast·→Africa/Indonesia¶ Tucana·Roast· → South·America¶
9. Move the right tab stop to the 3-inch mark.	
a) Verify that the paragraphs are all still selected.	Always important to maintain consistency.
b) Drag the right tab stop to the 3-inch mark.	Notice that as you drag, a dotted line appears in the document showing you where the text will align when you release the mouse. Type· → Region¶ Bogota·Supremo· → Colombia¶ Tarrazu· → Costa·Rica¶
10. Save the document.	An example follows.

The region information formatted using tabs

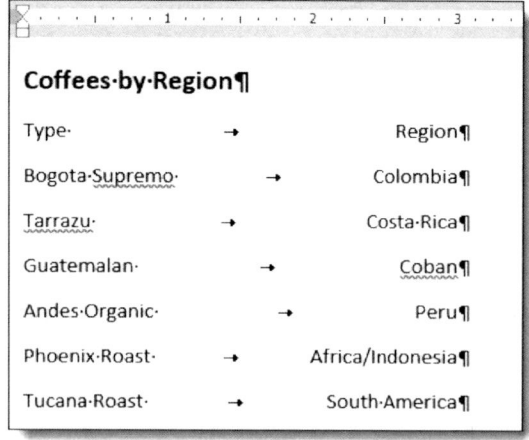

Setting tabs in the Tabs window

If you need more tab options than you get by setting tab stops on the ruler, you can use the **Tabs** window.

1. On the Home tab, in the Paragraph group, open the **Paragraph** window.
2. Click **Tabs**.
   The **Tabs** window opens.

   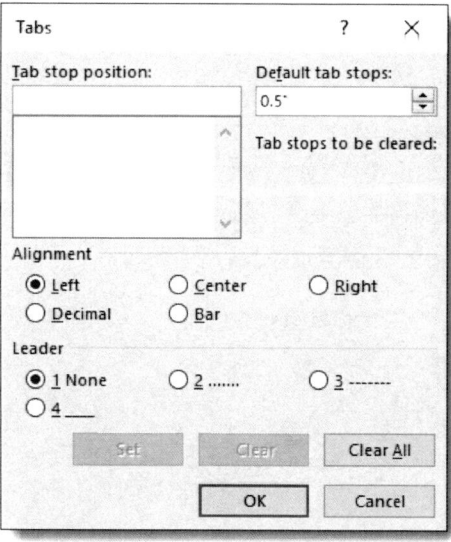

3. Set the options for each tab stop.
   a) Set the position in inches.
   b) Select the alignment and leader type.
   c) Click **Set**.
   d) Repeat for each tab stop you want to set.
4. You can also use the **Tabs** window to change the default tab stops for the current document.
5. When you are done, click **OK**.

Tab leaders

A *tab leader* is a repeating character that leads up to a tab stop, such as the row of periods that often appears between headings and page numbers in a table of contents. By default, tabs are set without leaders, but you can select from several leader types when you set tab stops in the **Tabs** window.

Tab stop with leader

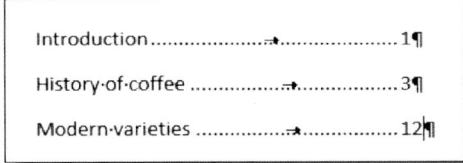

Clearing tab stops

You can clear tab stops by dragging them downward off the ruler. You can also clear all or individual tab stops from selected paragraphs by using the **Tabs** window.

1. On the Home tab, in the Paragraph group, open the **Paragraph** window.
2. Click **Tabs**.
    The **Tabs** window opens.
3. To clear an individual stop, select it from the list, and click **Clear**.
4. To clear all stops at once, click **Clear All**.
5. Click **OK**.

Exercise: Using the Tabs window to set tab stops

Coffee-tabs-formatted is open.

Do This	How & Why
1. Set a left tab at 1 inch for the coffee price list information.	Select all the paragraphs under the "Coffee Price List by the Pound" heading; activate the Left Tab icon; then click at the 1-inch mark on the ruler.
2. Insert tab characters as shown.	Insert two tabs in each line, one at the beginning, and one before the price.

Do This	How & Why
3. Select all the price list paragraphs, right-click, and click **Paragraph**.	To open the **Paragraph** window.
4. Click **Tabs**.	To display the **Tabs** window.
5. Add a decimal tab stop with a dot leader: a) In the position box, enter **3**. b) Under Alignment, click **Decimal**. c) Under Leader, click **2**.	A new stop is added at 3 inches, and you can see the results on the paragraphs because of the tab stops you entered. 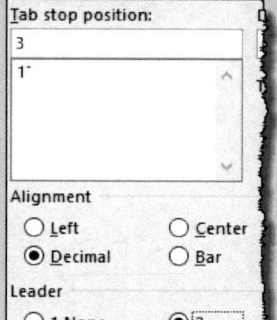
d) Click **Set**, and then click **OK**	
6. Observe the price list paragraphs.	The prices are now aligned on their decimal points, and there is a dot leader between the coffees and their associated prices.
7. Save and close the document.	

The coffee price list using dot-leader tab stops

Coffee·Price·List·by·the·Pound¶
→   Bogota·Supremo· ....→.........$9.75¶
→   Andes·Organic· ....→.........$11.25¶
→   Tarrazu· ....→................$10.50¶
→   Coban· ....→................$12.25¶
→   Phoenix·Roast ....→..........$12.00¶
→   Tucana·Roast............→............$14.00¶

Assessment: Formatting paragraphs

1. Indenting is a paragraph attribute. True or false?
   - True
   - False

2. What is it called when the first line of a paragraph is not indented, but the rest of the paragraph is indented?
   - Reverse indent
   - Inverse indent
   - Hanging indent
   - Outdent

3. What style can apply character and paragraph attributes at once?
   - Linked style
   - Combo style
   - Dual style
   - Charagraph style

4. Which tab-stop type aligns a decimal point to the stop?
   - Number stop
   - Column stop
   - Ledger stop
   - Decimal stop

5. What is the string of repeated characters called that leads up to a tab stop?
   - Tab leader
   - Tab line
   - Tab score
   - Tab tracer

6. The Tabs window provides more precision and more options than setting tabs on the ruler. True or false?
   - True
   - False

7. You can clear an individual tab stop by dragging it down off the ruler.
   - True
   - False

Module C: Quick Styles

Quick Styles provide styles for headings, emphasis, and body text. Unlike defined character or paragraph styles, Quick Styles change depending on the style set and theme that is applied.

You will learn:

- About Quick Styles, style sets, and themes
- How to apply Quick Styles
- How to use style sets and themes
- How to clear formatting

Character and paragraph styles

A set of text attributes taken together is called a *style*. Styles can be saved and then applied to text in order to change several attributes at once. Styles can also be copied using the Format Painter and applied to other text.

Exam Objective: MOS Word Core 2.1.2

Character style refers to a set of character attributes. *Paragraph style* is a collection of paragraph attributes. A *linked style* can change both character and paragraph attributes at once.

Quick Styles and themes

Quick Styles are sets of styles that are meant to go together for both function and formatting. Functionally, if you use Quick Style titles and headings, Word can create a collapsible outline in the navigation pane. You can then also change the look of all the text at once by changing the theme.

The difference between styles and themes is not immediately obvious, and there is some overlap in functionality.

- You change the style from the Styles group on the Home tab. Changing a style set changes the font, color scheme, and effects, including the alignment of some elements.
- You change the theme from the Design tab. Changing the theme changes font and color scheme, but not the effects or alignment.
- The Theme button provides options for changing the font and color scheme individually.

Using Quick Styles

Using Quick Styles allows you to take advantage of Word's theme and style features, as well as use document outlines.

Exam Objective: MOS Word Core 1.3.3, 2.2.6

1. Select the text you want to format.
   For title and headings, be careful to select all of the text to be formatted, including the paragraph mark. Other styles, such as Strong or Intense, can be used on individual words.
2. On the Home tab, from the Styles gallery, select the style you want.
   The gallery reflects the currently selected style set. You can use the arrow keys at the right end of the gallery to scroll through or open the gallery. If you point to a style, you will see a preview of how it will affect the selected text.

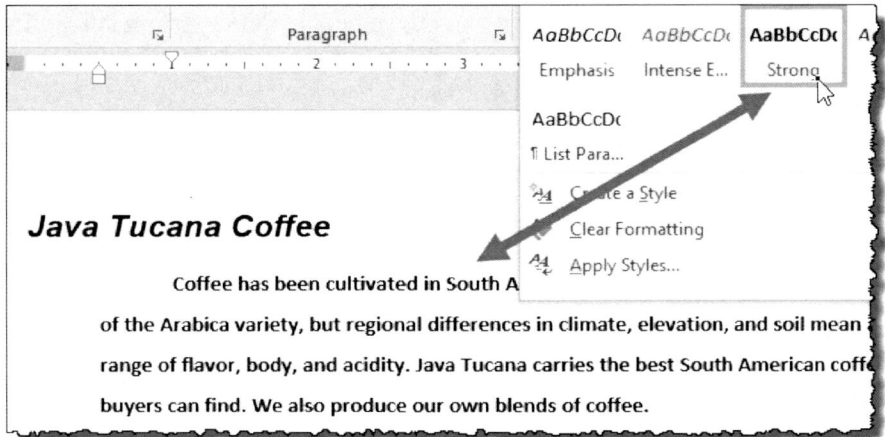

3. Repeat Steps 1 and 2 for other text.

You can use **Format Painter** to format multiple headings and other text.

Changing styles, themes, and other attributes

You can use Quick Styles to format headings and body elements, but you can quickly change the look of an entire document by changing the style set or theme. You can also quickly change other attributes, such as color, font, and paragraph spacing.

 Exam Objective: MOS Word Core 1.3.2, 1.3.3

- To change the style set, on the Design tab, select a style set in the Document Formatting group.
Changing the style set changes all the styles in your document in a single step.

- To change the theme, click the **Themes** button in the Design tab's Document Formatting group.

You can then select a theme from the gallery. After you've applied a theme, you can hover over theme options to see a preview. Themes control the colors, fonts, and other effects of the current style set.

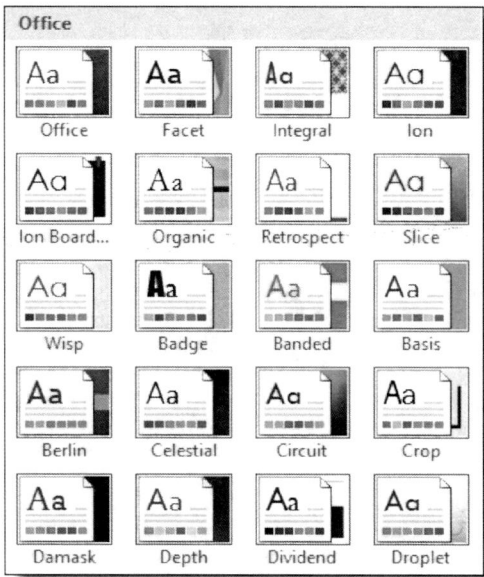

- You can further customize a theme (and thereby change the styles it governs) but using the Design tab's galleries for Colors, Fonts, Paragraph Spacing, and Effects.
    Note that the Effects button is for shapes and has no effect on text.

Clearing formatting

Sometimes you want to clear all previous formatting and start over with all text in the Normal, default style, which is Calibri, 11 points in Word 2016.

 Exam Objective: MOS Word Core 2.2.4

1. Select the text you want to return to default formatting.
    You can press **Ctrl+A** to select the whole document.

2. On the Home tab, click ⬚.
    In the Font group.

All formatting is removed, and text is returned to the Normal style.

Exercise: Using Quick Styles

 Exam Objective: MOS Word Core 1.3.2, 1.3.4, 2.2.4, 2.2.6

Do This	How & Why
1. Open JT-Coffee, and save it as JT-Coffee-QS.	From the Formatting text folder. The document is manually formatted with character attributes.

Do This	How & Why
2. Clear formatting in the document.	
a) Press **Ctrl+A**.	To select all the text in the document.
b) Click [icon].	The Clear All Formatting button is in the Font group on the Home tab.
3. Select the first line.	"Java Tucana Coffee."
4. On the Home tab, in the Styles gallery, click **Title**.	To apply the Title Quick Style to the text. It is now formatted as Cambria, 26 pt, and has a line beneath the paragraph.
5. Apply the Heading 1 style to "Single-region South American coffees."	Select the line, and click **Heading 1** in the Styles gallery.
6. Apply Heading 1 to "Java Tucana's blends."	Use the Style gallery or Format Painter. This paragraph is about halfway through the document.
7. Apply Heading 2 to the coffee variety and blend headings.	Apply Heading 2 to Brazilian Bourbon Santos, then double-click the Format Painter to apply the style to the other variety and blend names. When you finish using the Format Painter, press **Esc**. The result should look like this example. **Java Tucana Coffee** Java Tucana carries the best South American coffees our including our signature Tucana Roast. Here are some of t **Single-region South American coffees** Coffee has been cultivated in South America since the 17 differences in climate, elevation, and soil mean a wide ra **Brazilian Bourbon Santos** Brazil provides about a third of the world's coffee, and th this coffee is simple, smooth and agreeable.
8. On the Design tab, select a different Style set.	Use the gallery in the Document Formatting group. Style Sets change all of the styles you are currently using.
9. On the Design tab, click **Themes**.	To open a list of themes.
10. Point to different themes.	A theme preview is applied immediately to the page as you point to each.
11. Click **Badge**.	The document is changed, and the Document Formatting gallery reflects the look of the current theme.
12. Save and close the file.	An example follows.

The document with Casual style and Badge theme

Java Tucana Coffee

Java Tucana carries the best South American coffees our buyers can find. We also p[...]
including our signature Tucana Roast. Here are some of the coffees you can enjoy i[...]

Single-region South American coffees

Coffee has been cultivated in South America since the 1700's. Most of the plants ar[...]
differences in climate, elevation, and soil mean a wide range of flavor, body, and aci[...]

Brazilian Bourbon Santos

Brazil provides about a third of the world's coffee, and the best of that coffee is Bo[...]
this coffee is simple, smooth and agreeable.

Colombian Bogota Supremo

Rich and full-bodied, but with low acidity and a clean, sweet finish. Out of the many[...]
this is our favorite!

Assessment: Quick Styles

1. Both themes and styles can change which two attributes?

   - Font face/color
   - Font effects
   - Paragraph spacing
   - Heading colors
   - Paragraph alignment

2. The Document Formatting group allows you to change themes, colors, fonts, and paragraph spacing individually. True or false?

   - True
   - False

Module D: Making lists

Bulleted and numbered lists are types of paragraph formatting in which a bullet or number is applied to the beginning of each paragraph.

You will learn how to:

- Start a new bulleted or numbered list
- Promote or demote list items
- Use symbols as bullets
- Use pictures as bullets

Creating lists

You can create a bulleted or numbered list with AutoFormat or with ribbon commands.

Exam Objective: MOS Word Core 3.1.1

- To start a new bulleted list with AutoFormat, type * and press **Space** or **Tab**.
- To start a new numbered list with AutoFormat, enter 1. and press **Space** or **Tab**.
- To start a new list using the ribbon, click one of the list buttons in the Paragraph group on the Home tab.

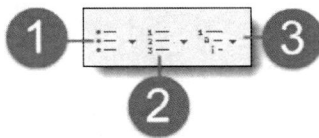

① *Bullets* apply a character such as a dot at the beginning of each list item.

② *Numbering* applies sequential numbers or letters to the items in the list.

③ A *Multilevel List* has an outline structure for the items.

- When you press **Enter** at the end of a list item, one of three things will happen:
  - If the current item is not empty, and new line will start with a bullet or number at the same level.
  - If the current item is empty and at the highest list level, the list will end and the paragraph will go back to a normal style.
  - If the current item is empty and not at the highest list level, it will be promoted.
- To apply bullets or numbering to existing paragraphs, select the paragraphs first, and then click the button for the type of list you want.

Exercise: Making a list

 Exam Objective: MOS Word Core 3.3.1, 3.3.4

Do This	How & Why
1. Open `French Press`, and save it as `French Press lists`.	From the current chapter's folder.
2. Select the five lines under the heading.	Don't select the heading.
3. On the Home tab, click the Numbering button.	The Numbering button is in the Paragraph group. The steps are numbered.
4. Press the right arrow key.	To move the cursor to the end of the last line.
5. Press **Enter**.	A new step starts.
6. Enter `Depress the plunger`.	
7. Add `Pour` as the final step.	Press **Enter** and type the text.
8. Press **Enter** three times.	The first time adds a new step, the second removes the number, and the third adds a blank line.
9. Type `Notes` and press **Enter**.	
10. Type * and then press the space bar.	A bullet list starts.
11. Create the following list items: • Heat water to 90-95C • Use course, dust-free grinds • Steep 2-3 minutes for small pots	
12. Press **Enter** twice.	To end the list. Compare your document to the one below.
13. Save and close the document.	

Using a French press

1. Heat water, but don't boil it
2. Grind coffee coarsely
3. Pour grinds into press
4. Pour water into press
5. Put lid on press and wait 4-5 minutes
6. Depress the plunger
7. Pour

Notes

- Heat water to 90-95C
- Use coarse, dust-free grinds
- Steep 2-3 minutes for small pots

List formatting

You can control the formatting of lists in a variety of ways.

- Promote and demote list items
- Change numbering formats
- Control where the numbering begins in a numbered list
- Change bullet formats
- Use other symbols as bullets
- Use pictures as bullets

Promoting and demoting list items

You can change the list level of an item from the ribbon or from the keyboard.

Exam Objective: MOS Word Core 3.3.4

- To promote or demote list items using the ribbon, select the items, and on the Home tab, in the Paragraph group, click the **Increase Indent** button or the **Decrease Indent** button.

- To demote (increase indent) a list item from the keyboard, place the cursor at the beginning of the line, and press **Tab**.
- To promote (decrease indent) an item from the keyboard, place the cursor at the beginning of the line, and press **Shift+Tab**. If the line contains no text, you can instead press **Enter**.
- To demote or promote multiple list items, select the items, and press **Tab** or **Shift+Tab**, respectively.

Using symbols as bullets

You can use a symbol, letter, or number from any installed font as a bullet. The Symbol and Wingdings font families are good resources for bullet symbols.

Exam Objective: MOS Word Core 3.3.2, 3.3.3

1. On the Home tab, in the Paragraph group, click the drop-down arrow on the Bullets button.

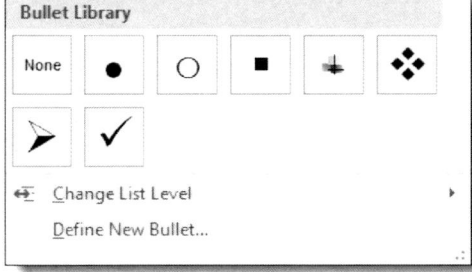

You'll see the Bullet Library, and might also see recently used bullets and document bullets, if you've used this feature before. You can click any of the symbols in the library to immediately apply it to the current level of the list.

2. Click **Define New Bullet**.

The **Define New Bullet** window opens. Here, you can define new bullet characters from any available font.

3. Click **Symbol**.

    The **Symbol** window opens.

4. Choose the symbol you want to use.

    a) Select a different font, if necessary.

    b) Select the symbol or letter, or enter the character code, if you know it.

    c) Click **OK**.

5. Click **OK**.

    You return to the document with the new bullet in place.

After you use a symbol once, it is automatically added to the bullet library.
You can repeat this process at different levels in the list hierarchy to change the symbol for all items at that level.

Using pictures as bullets

You can also use a picture file from the hard disk or from Office.com as a bullet symbol.

1. Click the drop-down arrow on the Bullets button, then click **Define New Bullet**.

    The **Define New Bullet** window opens.

2. Click **Picture**.

    The **Insert Pictures** window appears, giving you several choices for sources.

3. Select a picture source.

    - From a file: Click Browse next to this option to pick a file on your computer.
    - From SharePoint: If you are connected to a SharePoint server, you can use this option to select pictures from SharePoint.
    - Bing Image Search: Use the Bing search engine to find pictures online.

4. Select a picture and click **Insert**.

5. Click **OK** twice.

    To close both the **Picture Bullet** and the **Define New Bullet** windows.

    You return to the document with the new bullet in place.

After you use a picture once, it is added to the bullet library. You can repeat this process at different levels in the list to change the bullets for all items at that level.

Exercise: Formatting a list

Exam Objective: MOS Word Core 3.3.2, 3.3.3, 3.3.4

Do This	How & Why
1. Open `JT-Coffee-Service`, and save it as `JT-Coffee-Service-bullets`.	In the `Formatting text` folder.
2. Select the lines *between* Java Tucana Services and Java Tucana Coffee and Tea.	Do not select these headings.
3. Click [bullets icon].	The Bullets button is in the Paragraph group on the Home tab. The select paragraphs are now formatted as bullets.
4. In the list, select the three lines *between* "Cafés" and "Office coffee service."	
5. Click [indent icon].	One the Home tab, in the Paragraph group. The selected paragraphs are indented one level to the right, or *demoted*.
6. Select the items *between* "Office coffee service" and "Wholesale."	
7. Press **Tab**.	This is another way to increase the indent.
8. Increase the indent for the three items under Wholesale.	
9. Click on the item Wholesale.	To place the cursor there. You don't need to select it.
10. Change the symbol for bullets at this level:	
a) Click the drop-down arrow next to the Bullets button, and click **Define New Bullet**.	
b) Click **Symbol**.	
c) Select a Font.	Wingdings are good sources for bullets.
d) Select the character you want to use, and click **OK** twice.	All bullets at this level are changed.
11. Change the symbol for the bullets at the indented level.	Put the cursor in any item at this level, and change the symbol.
12. Use **Format Painter** to apply these bullets to items under Java Tucana Coffee and Tea.	The top level should be applied to "Single-region South American Coffees" and to "Java Tucana's blends." Everything else should be at the second level.
13. Save and close the document.	An example follows.

Word 2016 Level 1

Your document should look something like the following figure, with whatever symbols you chose.

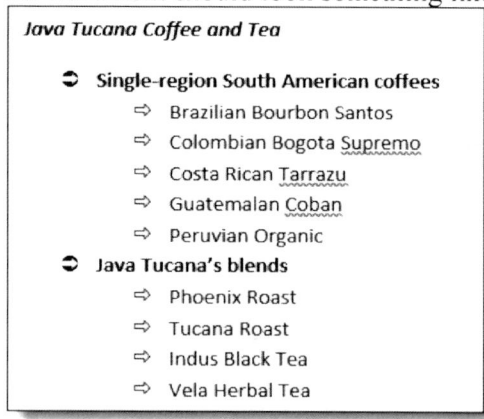

Changing numbering format in lists

You can easily change the format of the numbers in numbered list by using the Numbering Library gallery.

 Exam Objective: MOS Word Core 3.3.2

1. Select a paragraph at the level of the list you want to change.
2. Click the Numbering dropdown arrow, then select a format from the gallery.
   There are numbered and lettered options to choose from. To create a new number format, click **Define New Number Format**.

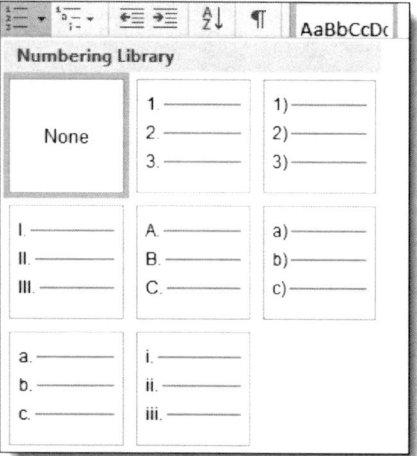

Controlling list numbering

You might sometimes find that a numbered list is continuing numbering from a previous list when you'd prefer that it start over. Or, you might have a list that you *do* want to continue from a previous one. You also might want a list to start from a particular number or letter. Here are some ways to control list numbering.

 Exam Objective: MOS Word Core 3.3.5, 3.3.6

- To cause a list to continue the numbering of the previous list, right-click one of the numbers in the list you want to change, and then click **Continue Numbering**.

- To start list numbering over from "1" (or "A" or "i," depending on your format), right-click a number and then click **Restart at 1**.
- To start list numbering from a specific number, right-click a number, and then click **Set Numbering Value**.

    You can then use the **Set Numbering Value** window to control whether this is a new list or a continuation, and what the starting value will be (by using the "Set value to" control).

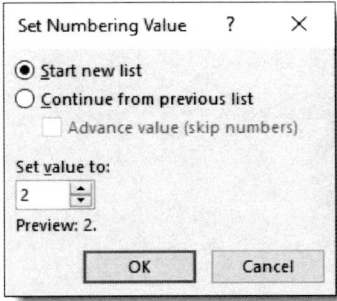

Exercise: Formatting numbered lists

Exam Objective: MOS Word Core 3.3.5

Do This	How & Why
1. Open Café Latté and save it as Café Latté Numbered.	This document contains a simple recipe for café latté. You will format it in a couple of ways to experiment with numbered lists.
2. Select all the paragraphs after "Prepare the milk".	
3. Click [numbered list icon].	To create a numbered list. This is ok, but we actually want "Prepare the latté" to be a heading, not part of the list.
4. Select **Prepare the latté**, then click [numbered list icon].	The text is no longer part of the list, but the list before it continues the numbering of the previous list. 1. Warm milk over medium heat. 2. Whisk the milk to a froth. *Prepare the latté* 3. Make a half cup of espresso for each cup. 4. Pour milk, but not foam, into each cup. 5. Spoon foam onto the top of each cup.
Continued...	

Do This	How & Why
5. Right-click within step 3, then click **Restart at 1**.	*(menu shown: Adjust List Indents…, Restart at 1, Continue Numbering, Set Numbering Value…)*
	Now the second list starts at 1. Sometimes, you will need to correct lists in this manner. If a list restarts numbering, but you want to continue the numbering from a previous list, right-click the step and click **Continue Numbering**.
6. Undo all the numbering you just did.	Click Undo several times. Now, you'll look at formatting options for a multilevel list.
7. Select all the paragraphs after the main heading, "Making Café Latté".	
8. Format the selected paragraphs as a numbered list.	Click *(numbered list icon)*.

9. Promote the steps under "Prepare the milk" and "Prepare the latté".	Select the steps, then click *(decrease indent icon)*. The document should look like this.
	
	1. Prepare the milk
	    a. Warm milk over medium heat.
	    b. Whisk the milk to a froth.
	2. Prepare the latté
	    a. Make a half cup of espresso for each cup.
	    b. Pour milk, but not foam, into each cup.
	    c. Spoon foam onto the top of each cup.

10. Observe the multilevel list options.	Select all the steps in the list, then click *(multilevel list icon)*. There are many options for multilevel lists.
	
	Current List
	1.
	  a.
	    i.
	
	List Library
	None 1) / a) / i) 1. / 1.1. / 1.1.1.

11. Press **Esc** to close the gallery.	
12. Save and then close the document.	

Assessment: Making lists

1. Which character do you type at the beginning of a line, followed by Space or Tab, to start a new bulleted list?

    - Period (.)
    - Asterisk (*)
    - Plus sign (+)
    - Hyphen (-)

2. You can use any character from any installed font as a bullet. True or false?

    - True
    - False

3. Which of the following are methods you can use to increase the indent level of (demote) a selected list item? Choose all correct responses.

    - Press Alt+Space
    - Press Tab
    - Press Alt+Tab
    - Click Increase Indent on the Home tab
    - Press Space

Summary: Formatting text

You should now know how to:

- Format characters by using the ribbon, and copy formatting using Format Painter
- Change paragraph attributes such as indents and line spacing, control indents, and set and use various kinds of tab stops
- Understand the different between character and paragraph styles, use Quick Styles to quickly format your documents, control the appearance of styles by using themes, and clear formatting
- Create bulleted and numbered lists, promote or demote items in a list, and control numbering format and bullet characters

Synthesis: Formatting text

1. Open `About Us` and save it as `About Us formatted`.
2. Format the following using Quick Styles:
   - The first line with **Title**
   - Java Tucana Services and Java Tucana Coffee with **Heading 1**
   - Headings under Java Tucana Services with **Heading 2**
3. Indent the entire service paragraphs by one-half inch.
4. Format the lists of coffees with bullets:
   - The top-level bullets should be "Single-region South American coffees" and "Java Tucana's blends."
   - Specific coffee names should be indented one level.

   Compare your document to the figure following the exercise.
5. Change the symbols used in both levels of the bulleted list.
6. Change any combination of styles, themes, colors, fonts, and spacing to achieve a look you like.
7. Save and close the document.

The document after step 3

Chapter 3: Document setup

You will learn how to:

- Change page layout settings, use columns, and control section breaks
- Check document spelling and grammar, and use AutoCorrect
- Print documents, and add and control headers and footers
- Base new documents on templates

Module A: Page layout

There are a number of ways to adjust page layout so that each new page looks the way you want at the start. The most commonly used of these options is setting the margin widths.

You will learn how to:

- Change margins
- Adjust pagination setting and add page breaks
- Change the way Word hyphenates
- Format text in columns
- Insert section breaks

Page layout

Most page layout settings can be managed on the Page Layout tab, and most of what you'll use is in the Page Setup group and window. Here you can set margins and orientation, set options for multiple pages (such as having facing pages mirror each other), select paper, and set options for sections, headers, and footers.

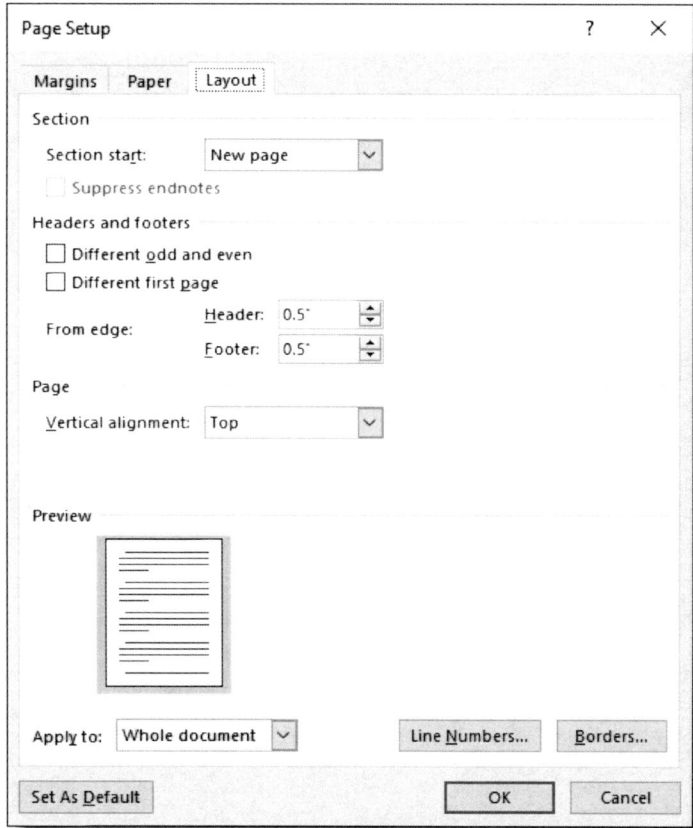

Other options can be set in the **Paragraph** window, which is available from both the Home and the Page Layout tabs.

Setting margins

You can select from a number of predefined margin widths, or you can define custom margins.

 Exam Objective: MOS Word Core 1.3.1

1. On the Page Layout tab, click **Margins**.

    A gallery of predefined margins opens.

    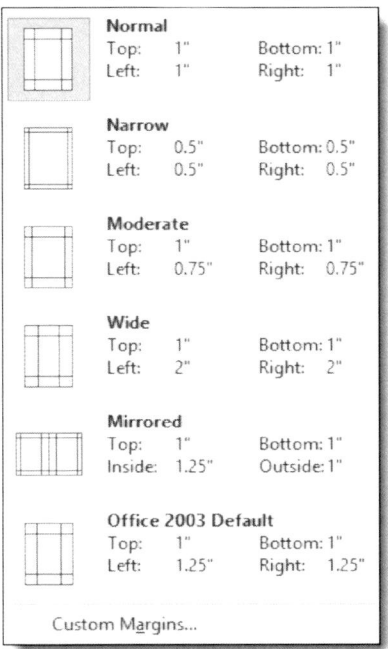

2. Select the margin layout you want.
3. If none of the predefined margins meets your needs, create your own:

    a) At the bottom of the margins gallery, click **Custom Margins**.
    The **Page Setup** window opens, with the Margins tab active.

    b) Enter values for the top, bottom, left, and right margins.
    To make your custom margins the default for all new documents, click **Set As Default**.

    c) Click **OK**.

The margins are adjusted for the document.

Adding breaks and non-breaking spaces

You can force line breaks without starting a new paragraph. You can also force page breaks or insert blank pages into a document. To see these normally hidden characters, click 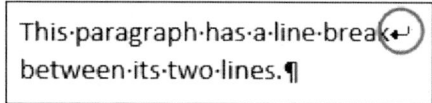 (the Show/Hide button) on the Home tab. Often, showing paragraph and space symbols can be very helpful in understanding exactly what is happening in your document.

 Exam Objective: MOS Word Core 1.4.6, 2.3.2

- To add a line break without starting a new paragraph, press **Shift+Enter**.

    If hidden characters are shown, the line break character looks like an Enter or Return symbol.

- To add a non-breaking space between words, press **Ctrl+Shift+Space**.

    This keeps words together and prevents a line break between them.

    If hidden characters are shown, the non-breaking space looks like a small circle at the top of the space, like this:

- To add a page break, press **Ctrl+Enter**; or on the Insert tab, click **Page Break**.

    If hidden characters are shown, you'll see a dotted line and the words Page Break:

    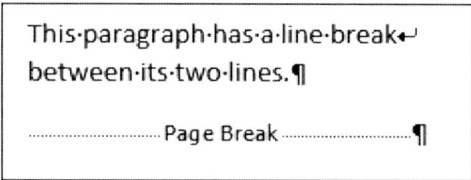

- To add a blank page, add two consecutive page breaks, or click **Blank Page** on the Insert tab.
- Like any other characters, you can remove line breaks, non-breaking spaces, and page breaks by deleting them.

Using hyphenation

By default, Word does not use hyphenation. If a word is too long to fit at the end of a line of text, it is automatically bumped down, or "wrapped," to the next line. You can add hyphenation manually or automatically.

Exam Objective: MOS Word Expert 2.1.3

1. On the Page Layout tab, click **Hyphenation**.

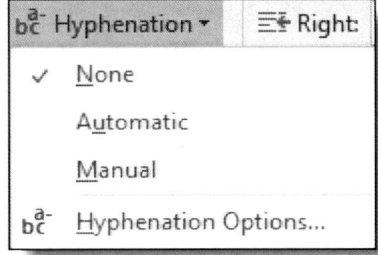

2. Click one of these options:

   - **Automatic** automatically hyphenates words that can be split.
   - **Manual** steps through the document and suggest words to be hyphenated. You accept, reject, or edit the suggestions.

   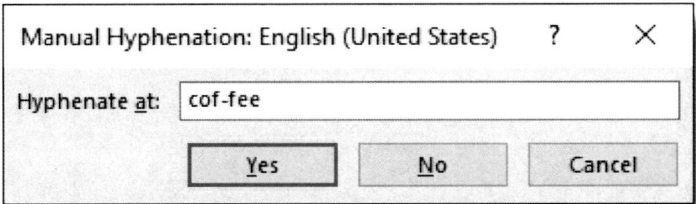

   - **Hyphenation Options** opens the **Hyphenation** window, where you can set automatic or manual hyphenation. You can also specify a maximum number of lines in a row in which a hyphen may appear, and a minimum distance from the edge that words should be hyphenated. Words that start closer to the edge than this are bumped to the next line, even if they could be hyphenated.

   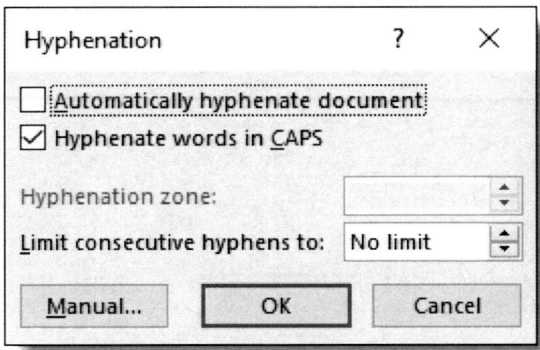

Showing line numbers

Sometimes, it's useful to show line numbers in a document, such as when proofing documents or when using them for legal purposes.

 Exam Objective: MOS Word Core 2.1.3

1. On the Layout tab, in the Page Setup group, click **Line Numbers**.

    To display the Line Numbers menu.

    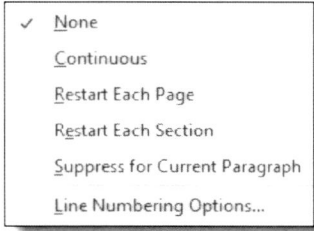

2. Click an option.

    You can have line numbers run continuously throughout the document, restart on each page, or restart for each section.

3. For more control, click **Line Numbering Options**.

Pagination

When the first line or last line of a paragraph is left alone on a page, it can be hard to read and looks bad. Word allows you some control over what happens when paragraphs cross page breaks. To use these options, select the paragraphs you want to adjust, open the **Paragraph** window, and click the **Line and Page Breaks** tab.

 Exam Objective: MOS Word Expert 2.1.5

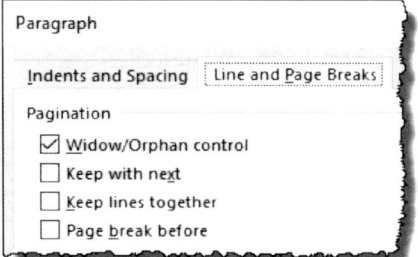

Here are the options you have under Pagination:

Window/Orphan control	Prevents first or last lines of the selected paragraph(s) from being left alone on a page. If the last line of a paragraph is by itself at the top of a page, Word pushes the second-to-last line down with it. If the first line of a paragraph is alone at the bottom of a page, Word pushes it down so the paragraph begins on the next page.
Keep with next	Keeps the selected paragraph on the same page as the next paragraph. This is useful for headings that should stay with the text that follows.
Keep lines together	Keeps all of the selected paragraphs on the same page.
Page break before	Inserts a page break before the selected paragraph.

Widow/Orphan control is enabled by default and applies to the whole document, but you can change settings for individual paragraphs.

Exercise: Changing basic page layout

 Exam Objective: MOS Word Core 2.1.3 and Expert 2.3.2

Do This	How & Why
1. Open `About JT`, and save it as `About JT Layout`.	From the current chapter's data folder.
2. Show symbols in the document.	If necessary. Click ¶ . It's useful to show symbols when doing any kind of document layout work.
3. Place the cursor at the start of the Java Tucana Coffees heading.	You will insert a page break so that this heading begins on a new page.
4. Hold down **Ctrl** and press **Enter**.	To insert a hard page break and force the heading onto the next page. The text now flows onto a third page.
5. Observe the hard page break symbol.	It is at the bottom of the previous page. Anything you type or enter after this symbol will go on the next page. To delete a hard page break, you simply delete this symbol. That's one reason why showing symbols is useful; without them, it can be difficult to tell exactly where the hard page break is.
6. On the Layout tab, click **Margins > Moderate**.	This makes the side margins a little narrower, allowing all the text to fit on two pages.
7. On the Page Layout tab, click **Hyphenation > Automatic**.	Several words in the document are now split across lines with hyphens.
8. Turn "Set hyphenation" back to **None**.	Hyphenation doesn't generally look good, and should only be used if saving every character of space is critical.
9. Save and close the document.	

Columns

You can format your document into two or more columns. Though the default values will often suffice, Word gives you control over the width of each column and the space between columns. As with other formatting options, columns can be applied to the whole document or only to the sections you want. Even without creating section breaks, you can specify that columns are applied only to selected text or only from the cursor location onward.

Creating simple column layouts

To use default setting and quickly format a document in columns, here's what you do.

 Exam Objective: MOS Word Core 2.3.1

1. Select the location where you want to have columns, or select the text that you want to format in columns.
2. On the Layout tab, click **Columns**.

    A gallery appears with several possible options.

    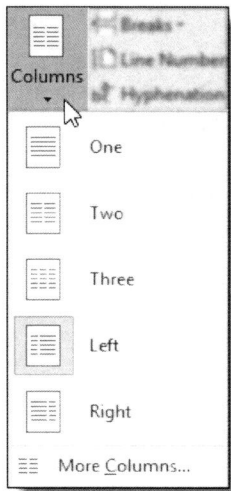

3. Click an option.

    - Click **One**, **Two**, or **Three** to create that many columns.
    - Clicking **Left** or **Right** will format the text in two columns with the left or right column bigger than the other.
    - For more control, click **More Columns** to display the **Columns** window. Here, you can choose the number of columns, set their width and the space between them, and add lines between them. You can also choose to apply the columns to the whole document, to selected text, or from the cursor location onward. The minimum width for a column is half an inch, so the number of columns you can fit on a page depends on the width of the page, the column spacing, and the margins.

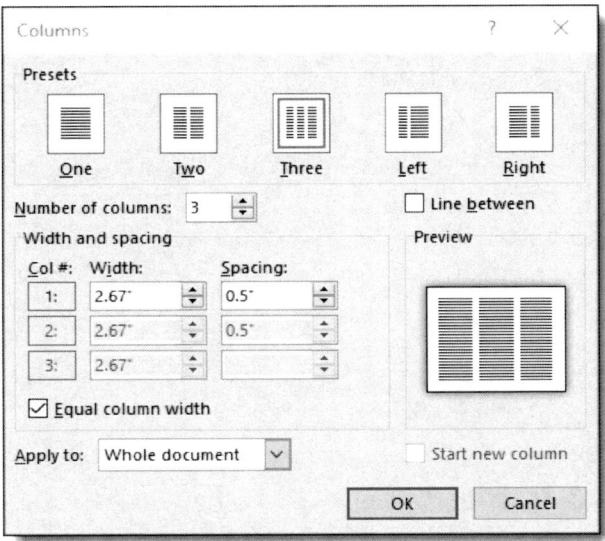

Inserting column breaks

To insert a column break, place the insertion point where you want it, then, on the Layout tab, click **Breaks**, then click **Column**.

Exercise: Using columns

 Exam Objective: MOS Word Core 2.3.1

Do This	How & Why
1. Open `Services` and save it as `Services Columns`.	This document describes Java Tucana services. The cursor should be at the top of the page.
2. Verify that symbols are showing in the document.	Click the Show/Hide button if necessary.
3. On the Layout tab, click **Columns > Two**.	The document is split into two columns. When you choose a column setting when the cursor is in flashing, the setting will apply to the entire section of the document. This document has just one section. You'll learn more about sections soon.
4. Place the cursor just before "South American Coffees."	Before the "S" but on the same line.
5. On the Layout tab, click **Breaks > Column**.	To force the text into the next column.
6. Undo the first two steps.	Press **Ctrl+Z** twice to return to the document as it was when you opened it.
Continued...	

Word 2016 Level 1   69

Do This	How & Why
7. Select the first three paragraphs and headings under Java Tucana Services.	Don't select the main heading.
8. Click **Columns > Three**.	The selection is split across three columns. Because these paragraphs are the same size, the headings ended up at the top of the columns. If they don't you can add column breaks to adjust the heading locations. See the example following the exercise.
9. Click **Columns > More Columns** and observe the options.	You can adjust the number of columns, column and spacing widths, and other options.
10. Click **Cancel**.	To close the window.
11. Put the South American coffees and their descriptions into two columns.	
a) Select the coffees and their descriptions.	Do not select the "South American Coffees" heading or the paragraph that follows it.
b) Click **Columns > Two**.	On the Layout tab. The coffees appear in two columns, but most of the text is in the first column.
12. Insert a column break before Costa Rican Tarrazu.	
a) Click before "Costa Rican Tarrazu".	
b) Click **Breaks > Column**.	The columns of coffee are better balanced this way.
13. Save but do not close the document.	

Formatting the Java Tucana South American Coffees section in two columns

South·American·Coffees·¶

Coffee·has·been·cultivated·in·South·America·since·the·1700's.··Most·of·the·plants·are·of·the·Arabica· variety,·but·regional·differences·in·climate,·elevation,·and·soil·mean·a·wide·range·of·flavor,·body,·and· acidity.·Java·Tucana·carries·the·best·South·American·coffees·our·buyers·can·find.·¶

Brazilian·Bourbon·Santos¶
Brazil·provides·about·a·third·of·the·world's· coffee,·and·the·best·of·that·coffee·is·Bourbon· Santos.··Always·a·good·choice,·this·coffee·is· simple,·smooth·and·agreeable.·¶

Colombian·Bogota·Supremo¶
Rich·and·full-bodied,·but·with·low·acidity·and·a· clean,·sweet·finish.··Out·of·the·many·fine· Colombian·coffees·we've·tried,·this·is·our· favorite!·¶

············· Column Break ·············

Costa·Rican·Tarrazu¶
One·of·our·most·flavorful·coffees—full·body,· rich·aroma,·and·acidic.··Strong·but·always· smooth·and·fragrant,·this·is·a·popular·choice·for· iced·coffee·and·other·frozen·delights.·¶

Guatemalan·Coban¶
Fruity·and·floral·with·a·hint·of·spice·and· moderate·acidity,·this·coffee·is·bright·and· complex.·¶

Peruvian·Organic¶
Organically·cultivated·along·the·Apurimac·River,· this·coffee·is·mellow·but·still·flavorful·and· aromatic.·¶

Sections

Understanding *sections* is very important to working effectively in Word. Many types of document setup—such as column layouts, margins, and headers and footers—are specific to a section of the document. A new document has only one sections, but you can insert section breaks when you want different document setup in different parts of the document. Some things you do—such as creating columns on only part of a document—automatically create sections.

Working with sections

When you want to create a new document setup of some kind in the same document, you will need to insert a section break. You can also specify that the status bar show the section number you are in.

Here are some ways to work with sections.

- Click ¶ to show symbols when working with multiple sections. This helps you to see exactly where the breaks are.
- To insert a section break, on the Layout tab, click Breaks, then click an option under Section Breaks. Next Page will start a new section on the next page, while Continuous will start a new section right where you are. The other two options allow you to have facing-page setups like in most books.

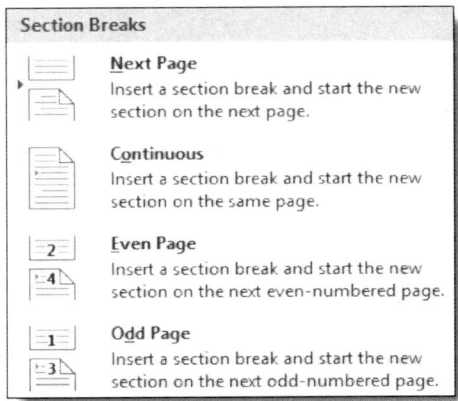

- To show the section number on the Status bar, right-click it and then click **Section**.

Exercise: Observing how sections work

Services Columns should be open.

Do This	How & Why
1. Verify that symbols are showing.	You should see paragraph marks, spaces, and other symbols in the document. If you don't, click the Show/Hide button on the Home tab. Symbols are very useful when working with sections and breaks.
2. Observe the section breaks in the document.	There is one after the first heading. This is because that heading is in a part of the document that has a single column, while the next section of the document has three columns.
3. Where are the other section breaks in the document?	There is one after the services columns, then one more before the columns of coffee descriptions.
4. Right-click the Status bar, then click **Sections**.	To show section numbers on the status bar.
5. Click in the **South American Coffees** heading.	You can see that this is Section 3 by looking at the Status bar.
6. Go to the end of the document.	Press **Ctrl+End**. This is Section 4.
7. Click **Breaks > Continuous**.	On the Layout tab. There is now a fifth section, which is set up in two columns. When you use a continuous section break, the new section inherits the layout of the previous one.
8. Undo the section break, and insert a next page section break.	
a) Click .	To remove the section break.
b) Click **Breaks > Next Page**.	Now, the new section begins on a new page. But it still inherits layout settings from the previous section, such as being in two columns.
9. Click **Columns > One**.	To specify that section 5 have just a single column.
10. Save and close the document.	

Assessment: Page layout

1. Which of the following key combinations will insert a page break?
   - Shift+Enter
   - Ctrl+Enter
   - Ctrl+P
   - Shift+Enter

2. By default, Word will not hyphenate long words over a line break. True or false?
   - True
   - False

3. What setting prevents first and last lines of a paragraph from being left alone on a page?
   - Changeling control
   - Line item control
   - Abandoned line control
   - Widow/Orphan control

4. What is the minimum width for a column in Word?
   - .25 inches
   - .5 inches
   - .75 inches
   - 1 inch

5. Section numbers appear on the Status bar by default. True or false?
   - True
   - False

Module B: Proofing documents

You will learn how to:

- Proof a document by checking its spelling and grammar.
- Use AutoCorrect and add AutoCorrect entries

Automatic spell checking

Word checks spelling and grammar continually and automatically by default. When it finds a possible error, Word underlines the word or phrase with a wavy line in either of two colors:

- Red indicates the word is misspelled or is not in the current dictionary.
- Blue indicates grammatical and typographic errors, such as two spaces between words. It also indicates a contextual spelling error—that the word is spelled correctly but is possibly not the word you meant. Examples would be using "your" when you meant "you're" or "it's" when you meant "its." Word's proofing options can also be set to check for issues such as sentence fragments, subject-verb disagreement, or run-on sentences; however, these options are not selected by default.

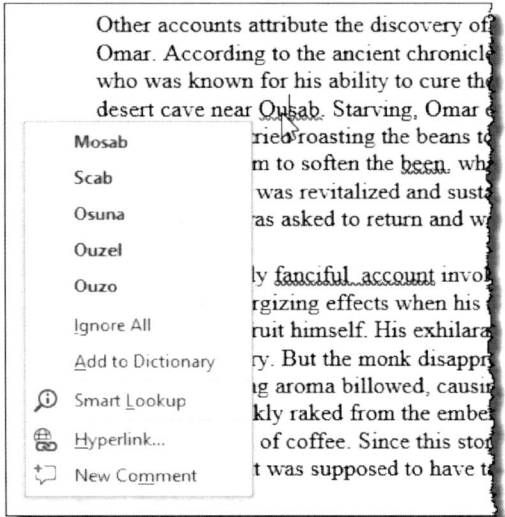

To address these issues, right-click the underlined text, and click the appropriate option. Word may suggest one or more terms, though it doesn't always have a suggested correction.

Sometimes, a proper name or an uncommon word will be flagged as a misspelling. In this case, you can choose to ignore all instances of the word in the document, or you can select and add the word to the dictionary, so that it is not flagged in the future. If you choose Ignore or Ignore All, and the underline will be removed.

Using the Spelling and Grammar panes

Although Word continually checks spelling and grammar on the fly, you might want to check an entire document at once, for instance, if you are editing or reviewing someone else's document.

1. On the Review tab, click **Spelling & Grammar**.
   The **Spelling** pane or **Grammar** pane opens, depending on the type of the first error found, if there is one.

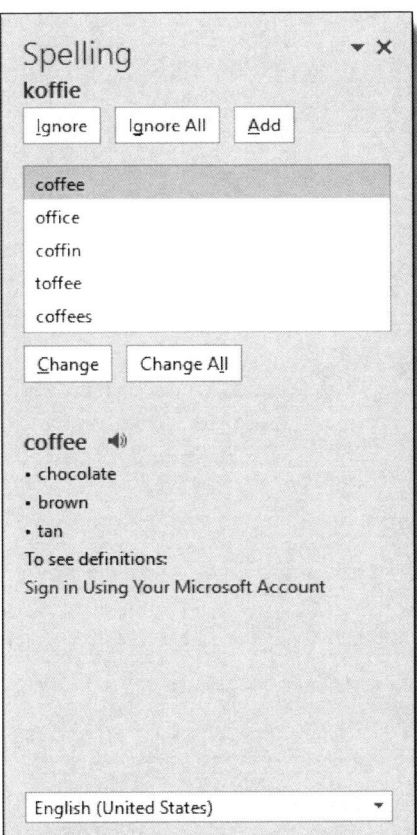 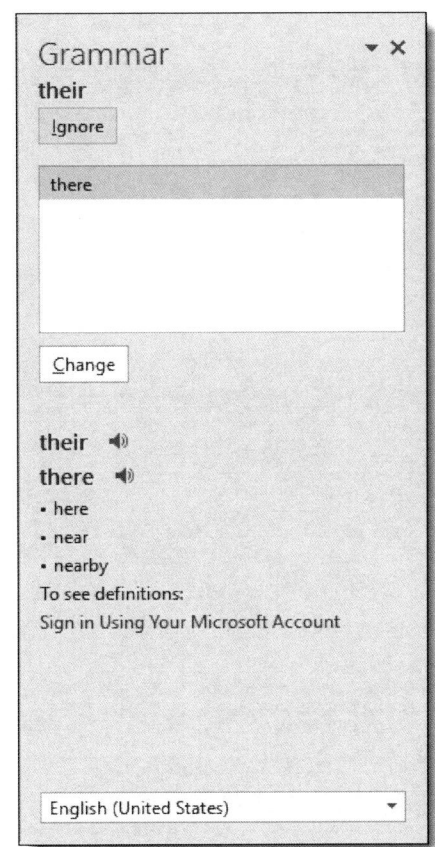

2. Take one of several actions:
   - Click **Ignore** to remove the underlining and move to the next issue.
   - Click **Ignore All** to remove the underlining from and ignore all instances of the term.
   - Click **Add** so that Word considers the term correct, even in other documents.
   - Select a suggestion, or edit in the window, and click **Change** or **Change All**.
     The **Options** button opens the Proofing options for Word, where you can change spelling and grammar settings.

Proofing options

To open proofing options, on the File tab, click **Options**, then click the **Proofing** category in the left pane.

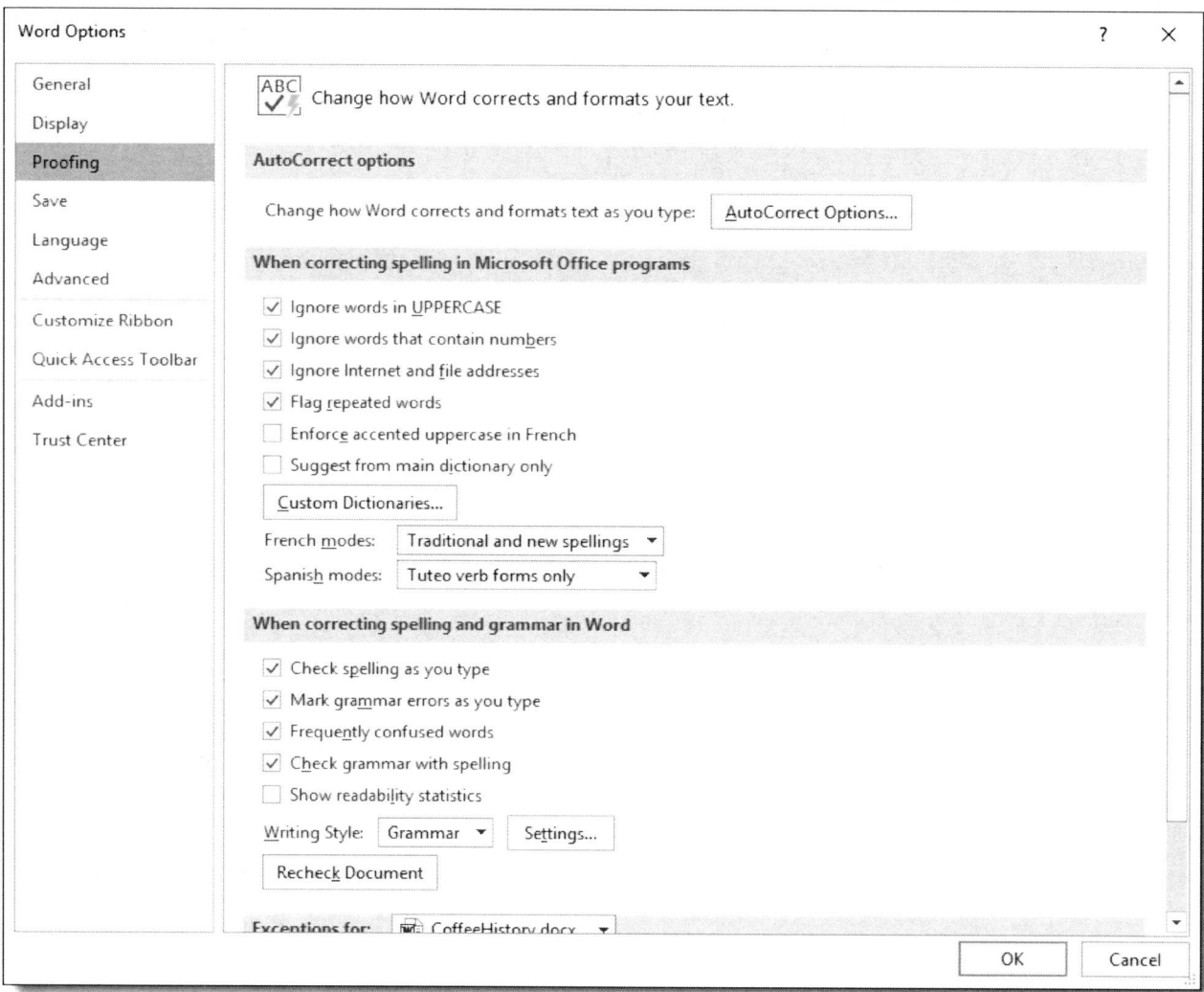

There are check boxes for many spelling and grammar options, as well as buttons to open AutoCorrect options, custom dictionaries, and grammar settings.

To change the language Word uses to proof a document, click **Language** on the Review tab.

Grammar settings

To open Grammar Settings from the Proofing options, click the **Settings** button.

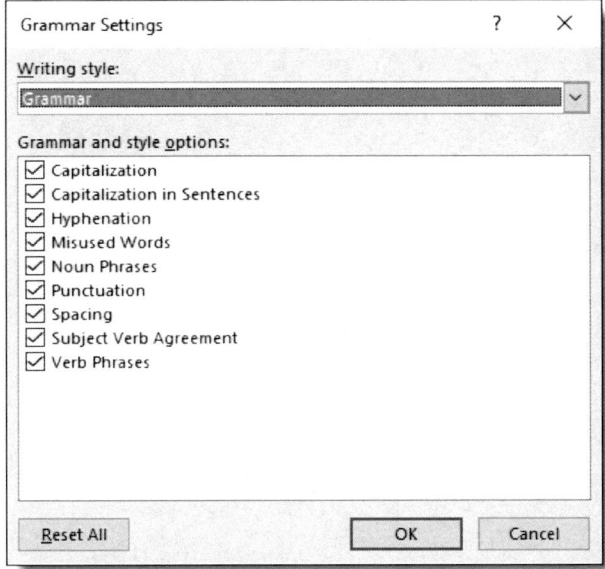

The **Grammar Settings** window provides options for both grammar and punctuation. By default, Word checks only for grammar issues such as proper capitalization, sentence fragments, and subject-verb agreement, among others.

Exercise: Proofing a document

Do This	How & Why
1. Open `Coffee in the Americas,` and save it as `Coffee in the Americas-ed.`	
2. Scan the document for errors.	You should see underlines in red and blue, indicating errors of spelling, and grammar and word choice, respectively.
3. At the end of the first full paragraph, right-click the word "their" underlined in blue.	A context menu provides another spelling option for this word ("there"). You can simply click on the suggested word to replace the error.
4. On the Review tab, click **Spelling & Grammar**.	To open the **Grammar** pane. It contains the two spellings, "their" and "there", and their definitions. The suggested replacement word, "there", is selected in the box.

Do This	How & Why
5. Click **Change**.	In the Grammar pane. The word is replaced in the sentence to correct it. The pane now shows the next issue that it found, and is now called the Spelling pane.
6. Observe the first spelling issue.	The Spelling pane shows that "Réunion" might be misspelled. But this is actually the name of an island and is correct.
7. Click **Ignore**.	To ignore the word and move to the next, "arabica", which needs to be capitalize.
8. Click **Change**.	To correct the error.
9. Continue to proof the document: a) Review each flagged item. b) If there is an error, select the right suggestion, and click **Change**. c) If the word is correct but unrecognized, click **Ignore**.	
10. When the spelling and grammar check is complete, click **OK**.	
11. Save and close the document.	

AutoCorrect

The term AutoCorrect is a bit of a misnomer: In many cases, AutoCorrect replaces a combination of common characters with characters or symbols that are not on a typical keyboard. For instance, the characters (c) are replaced by the copyright symbol.

 Exam Objective: MOS Word Core 2.1.3

To open the **AutoCorrect** window, in Backstage view, click **Options**, then click **Proofing**, and finally click the **AutoCorrect Options** button.

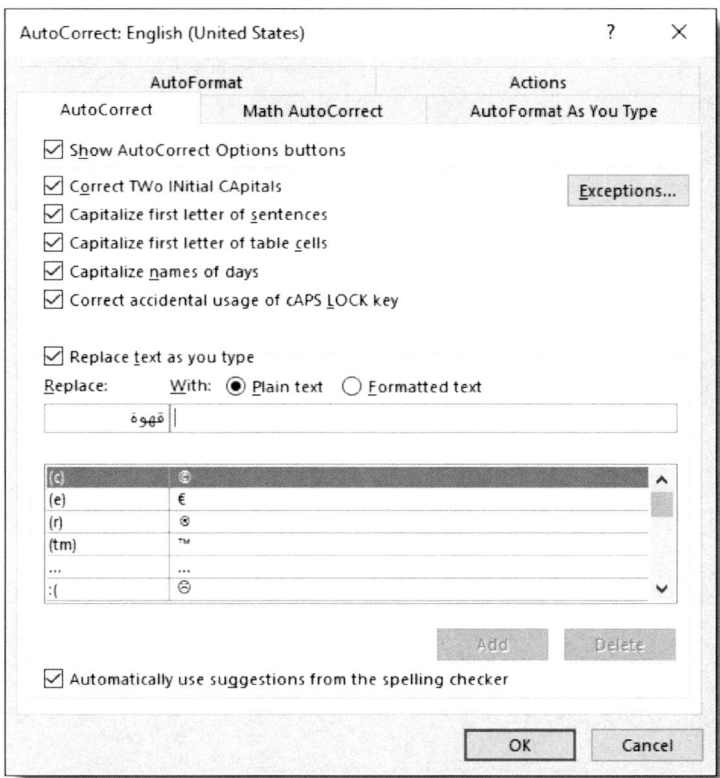

AutoCorrect capitalizes the first letter of a sentence. It also corrects instances of two capital letters starting the first word of a sentence, assuming this to be a mistake, such as "THe." You might want to add or remove exceptions for these rules, for instance, if there is a term you use that starts with two capital letters, or an abbreviation that ends in a period. Many abbreviations and the term "IDs" are already included in the exceptions.

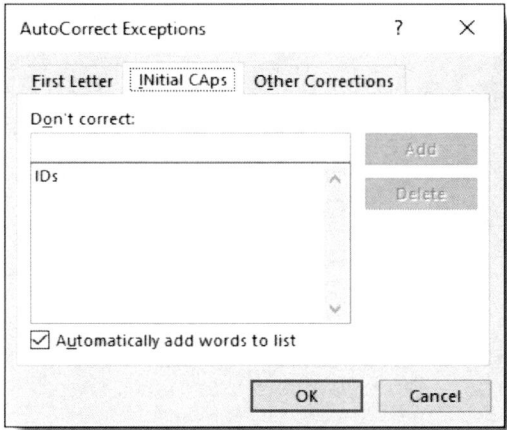

The **AutoCorrect** window also has tabs for AutoFormat and AutoFormat As You Type options. These options include such things as replacing straight quotation marks with angled quotation marks, and automatically starting numbered and bulleted lists when you begin a line with a number or asterisk, respectively.

The Math Autocorrect tab is specifically for mathematical symbols and formulas. The Actions tab allows you to add options to the right-click menu for text in a format that Word recognizes. For instance, if you right-click a date or phone number, you can access your calendar or contacts.

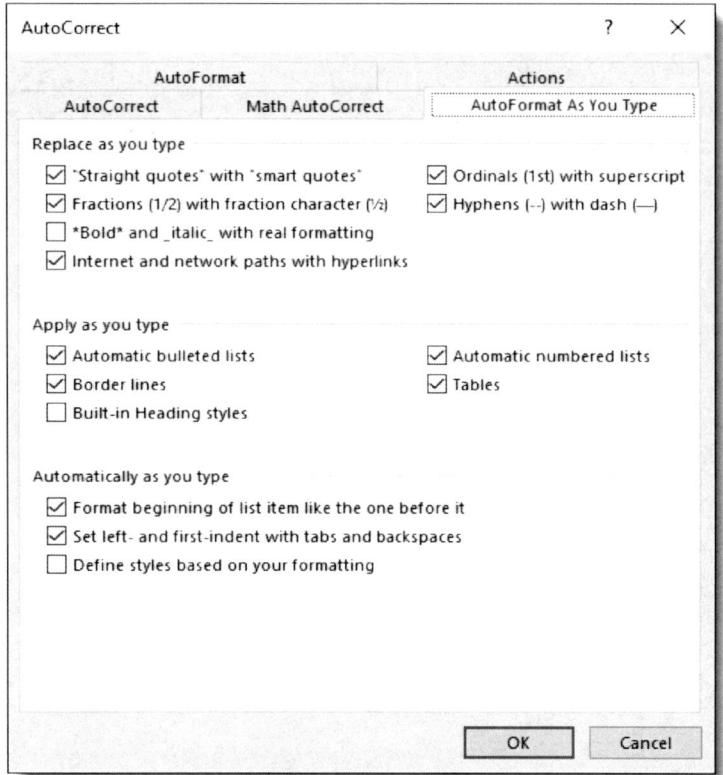

Although AutoFormat and AutoCorrect features are normally useful, there are situations in which the automatic replacements are an unwelcome nuisance, in which case you can turn off the corrections you don't want.

Creating an AutoCorrect entry

If you have text you type often, such as your full name, your company's address, or a descriptive product paragraph, you can create an AutoText entry to quickly enter that text when you type an abbreviation.

1. Display the AutoCorrect Options window.
2. Under Replace text as you type, enter the abbreviation you want to use under Replace, and the text to replace it with under With.
3. Click **Add**.

The entry will be added to the AutoCorrect feature. If you type the abbreviation and then press **Enter** or the spacebar, AutoCorrect will enter the full text for you.

Exercise: Using AutoCorrect

Do This	How & Why
1. Open a new, blank document.	You'll use this to experiment with AutoCorrect.
2. Type `the` and press **Enter**.	Be sure not to capitalize it. As soon as you press Enter, Word capitalizes "The". This is an example of Word's AutoCorrect feature, which will automatically fix many types of spelling and grammar mistakes you might make. But what if you had *wanted* "the" to be uncapitalized?
3. Click ↶ .	To undo the automatic "correction". When you don't like what AutoCorrect does, just click Undo.
4. Type `teh`, then a space.	Word changes what you typed to "the". When you type a common misspelling like this one, then press either the spacebar or Enter, Word will often correct it. You can also add your own common misspellings, or use AutoCorrect to create typing shortcuts.
5. Create an AutoCorrect shortcut for "Java Tucana".	
a) In Backstage view, click **Options**, then click **Proofing**.	To display Word's proofing options.
b) Click **AutoCorrect Options**.	To display the AutoCorrect window. Here, you can control the rules AutoCorrect uses and manage the AutoCorrect "Replace text as you type" entries.
c) In the Replace box, type `JT`.	You will use this abbreviation for the company name, "Java Tucana".
d) In the With box, type `Java Tucana`.	
e) Click **Add**.	To create the AutoCorrect entry.
f) Click **OK** twice.	To return to the document.
6. Type `JT`, then press the spacebar.	AutoCorrect replaces "JT" with "Java Tucana". This is useful for text you type often.
7. Close the document without saving it.	

Assessment: Proofing documents

1. Word always suggests at least one option for an incorrect word or phrase. True or false?

   - True
   - False

2. Which option do you choose when you want Word to remember a spelling, even for future documents?

   - Change All
   - Ignore All
   - Add or Add to Dictionary
   - AutoCorrect

3. What is the feature that can automatically replace a combination of common characters with other characters or symbols not typically found on your keyboard?

   - AutoChar
   - AutoReplace
   - AutoFormat
   - AutoCorrect

4. What feature is responsible for starting a new numbered list when you start a line with a number?

   - AutoFormat
   - AutoCorrect
   - AutoList
   - AutoNumber

Module C: Printing, headers, and footers

Although you will probably share many documents electronically, you will also sometimes need to print documents. For any document longer than three or four pages, it's useful to have headers or footers to show the current page number, document and chapter titles, creation date, and other information.

You will learn how to:

- Print a document and control print settings
- Add and edit headers and footers
- Use different first page or odd and even page headers and footers

Printing

While a lot of document sharing is now done digitally, sometimes you might need to print a document. To see the print options, click Print on the File tab.

Exam Objective: MOS Word Core 1.5.3

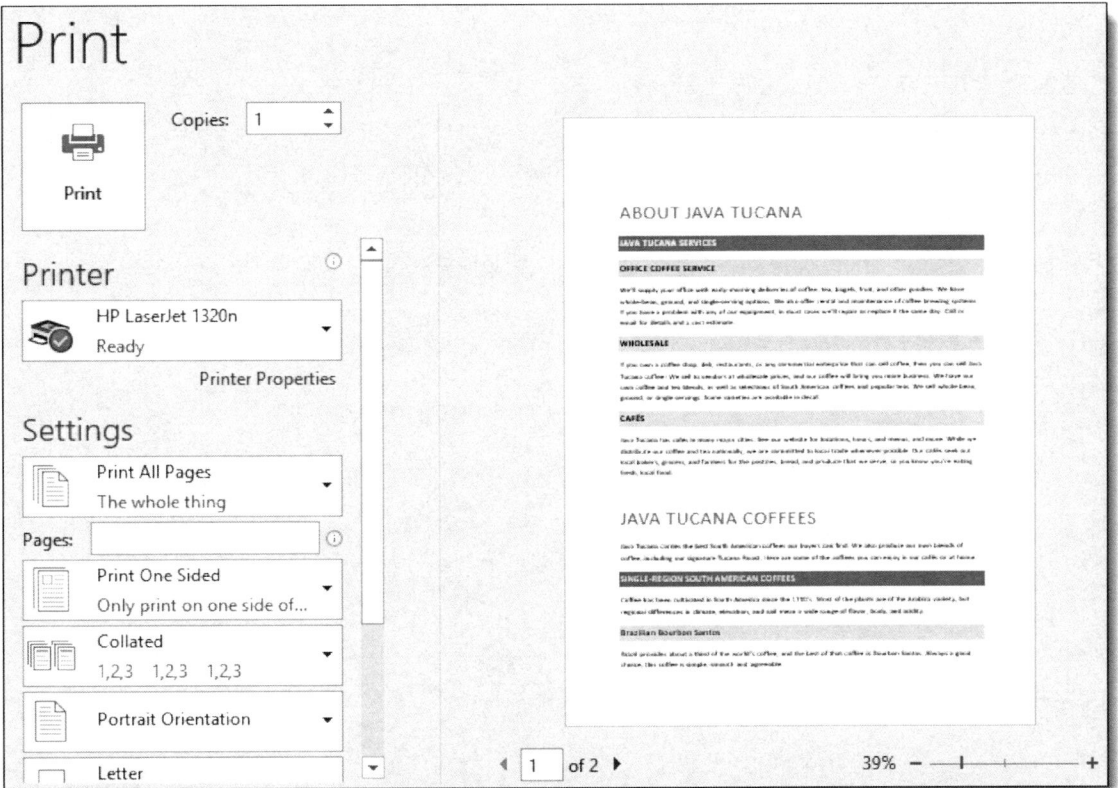

Microsoft automatically installs a software document writer, even if you don't have a physical printer, so the print function will always be available. Depending on what other hardware and software you have installed, you might be able to print to multiple printers, or directly to PDF or graphics files.

The print preview shows you what the output will look like. You can flip through the pages and zoom in an out.

Word 2016 Level 1

Modifying print settings

There are many option on the left of the Print screen.

 Exam Objective: MOS Word Core 1.5.1

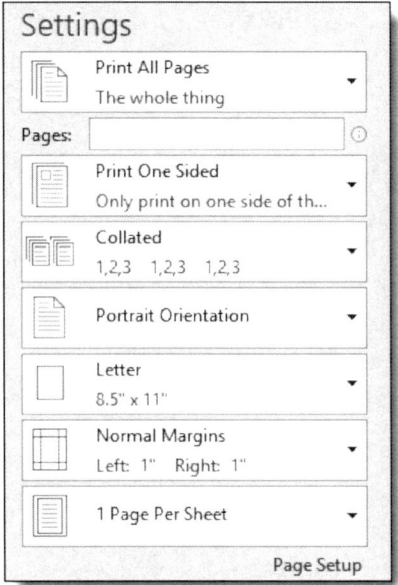

1. Click **File > Print**.

    The Print screen appears, giving you many options for modifying print settings.

2. Select the options you want.

    - Print all pages, the current one, a selection, or a range of pages.
    - Some printers can print on both sides of the page automatically. If your printer has this feature, the option will be available. Otherwise, you can choose to print on both sides of the page by manually flipping the output and feeding it back into the printer.
    - Some printers give you collation options.
    - Orientation controls whether the document will print tall (*portrait*) or wide (*landscape*).
    - Paper size.
    - Margins.
    - Page per sheet.

Exercise: Exploring printing options

Exam Objective: MOS Word Core 1.5.1, 1.5.3

Do This	How & Why
1. Open `JT Info` and save it as `JT Info Printing`.	The document contains information about Java Tucana.
2. Click **File > Print**.	The print screen appears in Backstage view. A preview appears on the right, and a gallery of print settings options on the left.
3. Click the preview, then press **Page Down**.	In this way, you can move through the pages of the preview to see what the document will look like when you print it.
4. Click the dropdown arrow next to Print All Pages.	You can print all pages, a selection, the current page, or document information.
5. Click the orientation dropdown arrow.	You can print the document portrait (tall) or landscape (wide).
6. Observe the other print settings.	The options available will depend on your current printer.
7. Return to the document.	Press **Esc** or click the return arrow.

Headers and footers

The header and footer put the same content on each page, though there are options to make the first page different, and to make even and odd pages different.

Exam Objective: MOS Word Core 1.3.4

To add or edit content in the header/footer area, you have to open it for editing. Header and footer areas always open together; that is, you won't open only one or the other for editing. There are three ways to open the header/footer for editing:

- Double-click the header or footer area on any page.
- Right-click the header or footer area, and click **Edit Header** or **Edit Footer**. They both open, regardless of which you choose.
- Use one of the header or footer options on the Insert tab.

When the header and footer area is open, you see a Header & Footer Tools/Design context tab. You can do a lot right from here.

Think of the header and footer areas as small documents. When the header/footer area is open, the functions on other tabs are still available, so most of the things you can do in the main body, you can also do in the header and footer. Here are some things you can do with headers and footers:

- Add text, pictures, tables, and other elements.
- Insert fields to display page numbers, the current date and time, and other information.

- Format header content using the font and paragraph tools on the Home tab, as you would any text. This includes character formatting, lists, alignment, and indenting.
- When the header and footer are open, use the ruler to set margins, indents, and tab stops that are different than those in the main document.
- Control the position of the header and footer user tools in the Position group of the Header & Footer Tools Design tab.

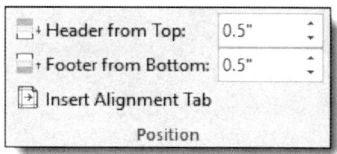

- Make the headers and footers different on the first page, and different on even and odd pages. Select the check boxes on the Header & Footer Tools tab, and edit the different headers accordingly.

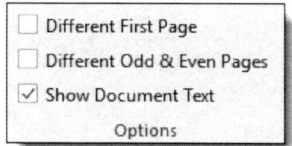

- Click the **Header** or **Footer** button in the Header & Footer group to choose from a gallery of complete built-in headers and footers, which have sets of elements in different styles. You can also save your own headers and footers to the galleries.

To remove a header or footer you don't want, click **Header** > **Remove Header** or **Footer** > **Remove Footer**.

Adding page numbers

Adding a page number field to the header, footer, or side margins ensures that each page automatically has the right page number. You can choose from many locations and styles, and you can format these numbers as you would any text.

 Exam Objective: MOS Word Core 1.3.5

1. Double-click in the header or footer area of any page.
   To activate the Header & Footer Tools Design context tab.
2. Click **Page Number**, and then click the general location where you want the page numbers.
   To open the page number gallery for that location.

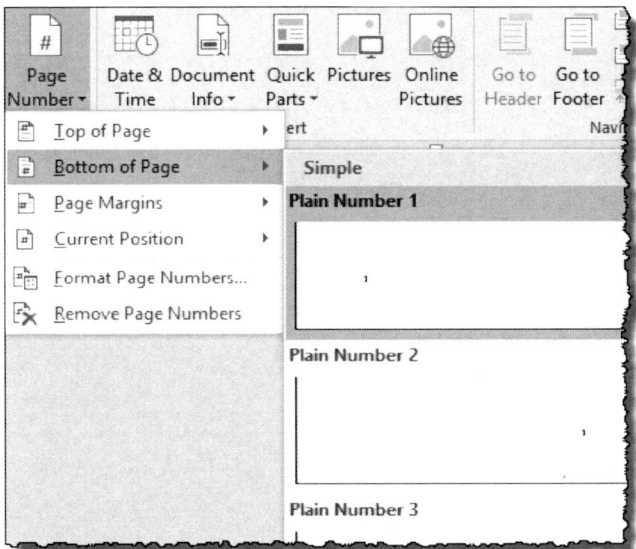

3. Select the number style you want.
    Scroll down the gallery.

    The number is added where you specified, in the style you selected. You can repeat the process to add page numbers in more than one place, if you want.

4. To remove page numbers, click **Page Number > Remove Page Numbers**.

Formatting page numbers

In addition to the locations and styles you can choose from, you can format page numbers in a couple other ways. With the header/footer sections active for editing, format page numbers as follows:

- Click **Page Number > Format Page Numbers**.
    This opens the **Page Number Format** window, where you can change the format from numbers to letters or Roman numerals. You can also include chapter numbers or change the starting page number.

    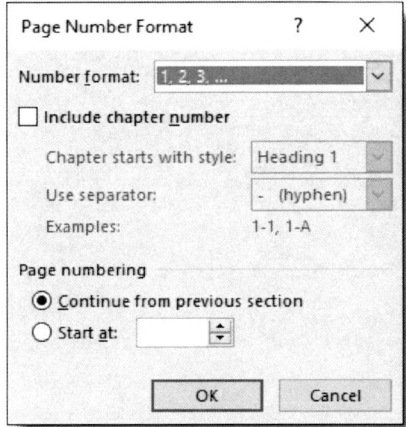

- You can select the page number text on any page and use the formatting options available on the Home tab, such as font face, size, color, style, and text effects.
    Formatting you apply to any page number is applied to all page numbers in the same header or footer location.

Adding the date and time

You can add the current date and time to the header or footer.

1. Double-click in the header or footer area of any page.
   To edit these areas and activate the Header & Footer Tools tab.
2. Click **Date & Time**.

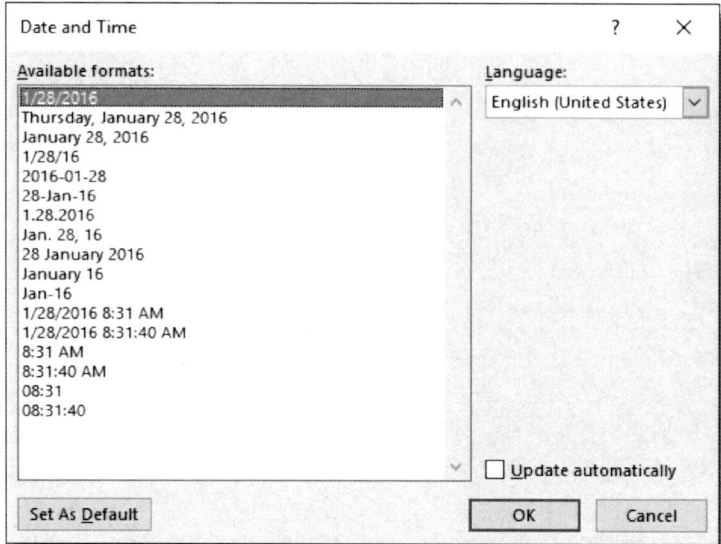

3. In the **Date and Time** window, select the format you want.
4. Check or clear the **Update automatically** check box.
   If you don't use this option, the date will be static text. If you do, Word will keep changing the date to the current date when you save the document. To update the date while the document is open, click it and then click **Update**.

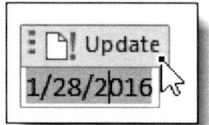

5. Click **OK**.
   The current date and/or time appears.
6. Format the date and time text.
   You can format all or part of the date and time by selecting the date and time text on any page and using the format options on the Home tab, such as font face, size, color, style, text effects, and alignment. Formatting you apply to the date and time on any page will be applied to the date and time on every page.

Using built-in headers and footers

Word comes with several built-in headers and footers. These have different elements and styles. You can use these as-is or start with one and edit it. After you create a header that you like, you can save it as a custom built-in header for future use.

1. Double-click in the header or footer area you want to edit.

    To open the areas for editing and display the Headers & Footers Tools tab.

2. Click **Header** or **Footer**.

3. Scroll down the Built-in gallery and select the header or footer you want.

    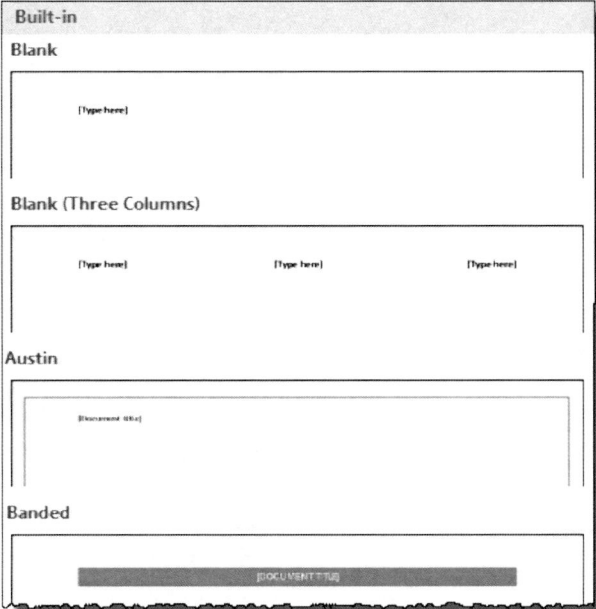

    The header or footer is inserted. You can edit this if you want.

4. You can save a header or footer you created or edited for later reuse:

    a) With the cursor in the header or footer, press **Ctrl+A** to select all.

    b) On the Header and Footer Tools tab, click **Header > Save Selection to Header Gallery** or **Footer > Save Selection to Footer Gallery**.

    The **Create New Building Block** window opens.

    c) Enter a name, and click **OK**.

    The header or footer now appears in the corresponding built-in gallery.

Exercise: Adding headers and footers

JT Info Printing is open.

 Exam Objective: MOS Word Core 1.3.4, 1.3.5

Do This	How & Why
1. Observe the Header option on the Insert tab.	Click Header to view the gallery. Word has many build-in headers that you can insert simply by clicking an option here.
2. Double-click at the top of the page, in the header area.	The header area is activated, and the rest of the document is faded. The Header & Footer Tools become available. You'll add a page number and some text to the header area.
3. On the Header & Foot Tools Design tab, click **Page Number > Top of Page > Plain Number 2**.	A page number is place in the middle of the header.
4. Just before the page number, type `About Java Tucana` .	Include a space at the end.
5. Select all the text in the header.	About Java Tucana **1**
6. On the Home tab, change the font to Arial, 12-pt.	You can format header text as you would any other text.
7. On the Header & Footer Tools Design tab, click **Close Header and Footer**.	The header is closed and the main document is active. You could also have double-clicked in the document area.
8. Scroll down and observe the numbers.	They change on each page.
9. Add the date to the footer.	Double-click the footer; then, on the Design tab, click **Date & Time**; click a format of your choosing and click **OK**; and then close the footer area.
10. Save the document.	

Different first or odd and even page headers and footers

Often you won't need a header on the first page of a document (because you have the title there already). And if you're publishing a document in a book format, you'll probably want different alignment of the headers and footers on the odd and even pages. Use the settings in the Header and Footer Tools Design tab's Options group to specify these settings. Then, you can create a separate header and footer for the first page, odd pages, and even pages.

Also note that headers and footers are specific to sections. If you need to have the headers change once you get to the beginning of a new chapter, for example, you can create a new section, then create all new headers and footers for it.

Exercise: Using different headings for the first page or for odd and even pages

JT Info Printing is open.

Do This	How & Why
1. Observe the header on the first page.	It's not really necessary. Usually, a first page has a title, and we already *know* it's the first page.
2. Activate the Header and Footer areas.	Double-click them, if necessary.
3. In the Options group, click **Different First Page**.	Now the header is identified as the First Page Header, and is blank. Of course, the first page footer is now blank as well, and you might want to enter the date there.
4. Click **Different Odd & Even Pages**.	In the Options group of the Header & Footer Tools Design tab. Now you can create different odd and even pages, to make the document look good when printed as a booklet or book.
5. Insert an even page header for the even pages.	
a) Click in the Even Page Header box.	You'll need to scroll down to the second page.
b) On the Insert tab, click **Header**.	To display the gallery of header options.
c) Click **Motion (Even Page)**.	To insert this header entry. Notice that it is left-aligned (even pages are on the left in a book).
6. Insert the Motion (Odd Page) header for odd pages.	Click in the Odd Page Header box on page 3, then, on the Insert tab, click **Header** and then click **Motion (Odd Page)**.
7. Preview the printed document.	You'll see that the headers on pages 2 and 3 are aligned oppositely, which looks good. You'll also notice that the date footer is appearing only on odd pages. You'd want to fix that before actually printing.
8. Save and close the document.	An example follows.

The previewed document showing different odd and even headers

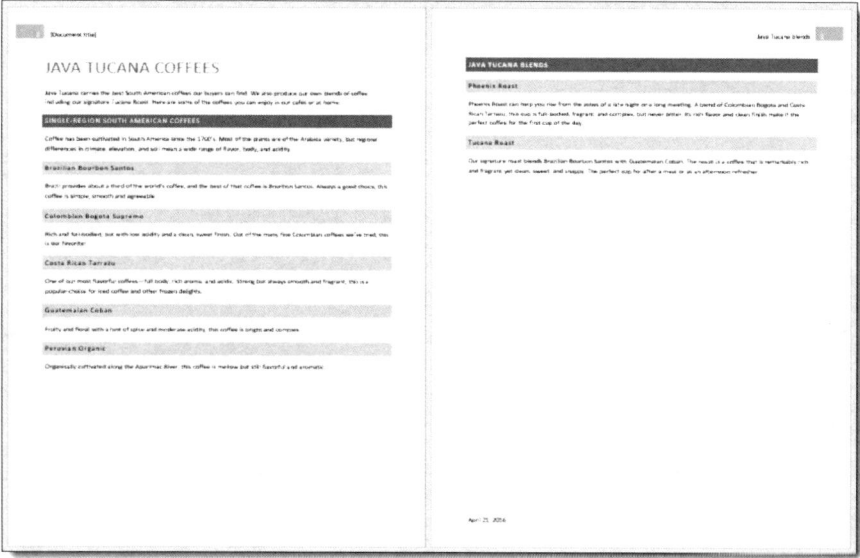

Assessment: Headers and footers

1. Which of the following techniques will open the header and footer areas for editing? Choose the single correct answer.

    - Press Ctrl+H
    - Press Ctrl+Alt+H
    - Double-click the header area
    - Press Ctrl+Alt+F

2. Page number fields automatically update as you add or delete pages. True or false?

    - True
    - False

3. By default, a header will not print on the first page of a document.

    - True
    - False

Module D: Templates

There is a staggering number of Word templates available for everything from mailing labels to memos to menus. The biggest challenge is not finding what you need, but choosing from the possibilities.

You will learn how to:

- Find, download, and apply a template from the web
- Apply a local template file

Templates

Templates provide the default formatting and layout for a new document. A template can have a specific purpose, such as a resume or an invoice, or it can be more general-purpose. Every document uses a template. The template that opens by default in Word is called the Normal template. It has 1-inch margins and uses 11-point Calibri as the default font for body text. It uses various other fonts for headings.

There are many templates for many purposes available in Word and online. The figure shows a few of the templates from Office.com, and gives you suggestions for searches. These can be accessed when you create a new document.

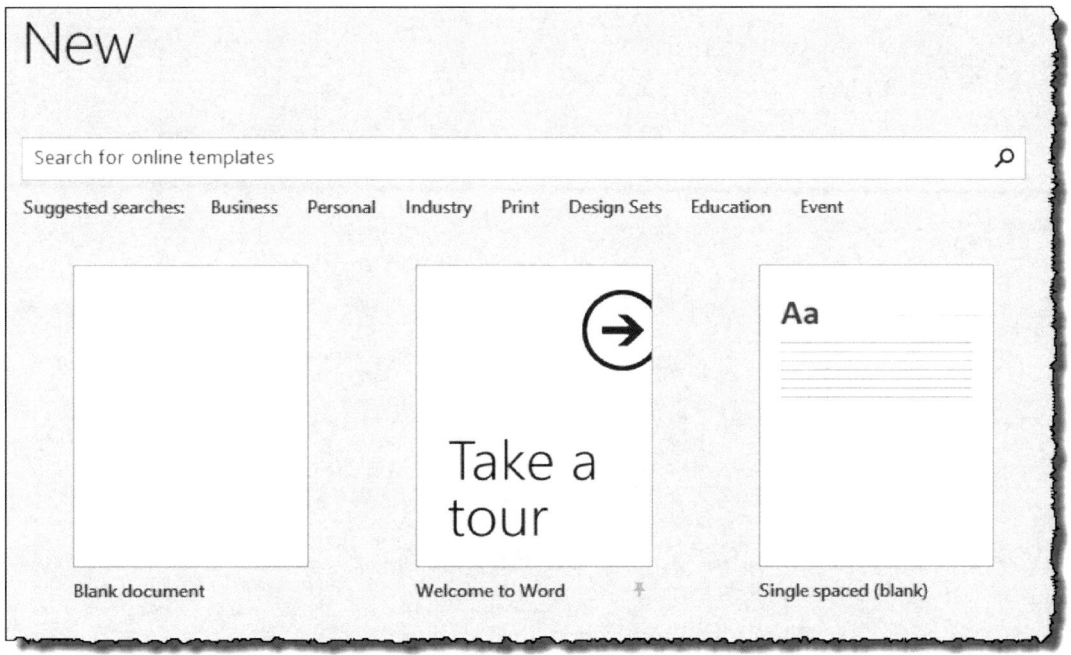

Template file names for Word have a .dot or .dotx extension. Templates that you create or download outside of Word and store on the local hard disk can be opened directly from Word or Windows explorer. When you store then in the default templates folder, you can access them from the New screen in Backstage view.

Applying templates from the web

The **New** command of the File tab provides access to templates. In addition to any templates you may have stored locally, there are many available from Office.com that you can access through searches.

Exam Objective: MOS Word Core 1.1.2

1. On the File tab, click **New**.

    You will see some templates from which you can choose, along with a search box and links for suggested searches. If you have saved your own templates, you will see a link for accessing those.

2. Click a suggested search.

    The Business category has many useful templates.

    You will see a list of found templates, and a list of sub-categories on the right.

3. Browse to locate a sub-category of templates that fits your requirements.

    Here, you see a list of available Business Plan templates. There are literally thousands of templates available online.

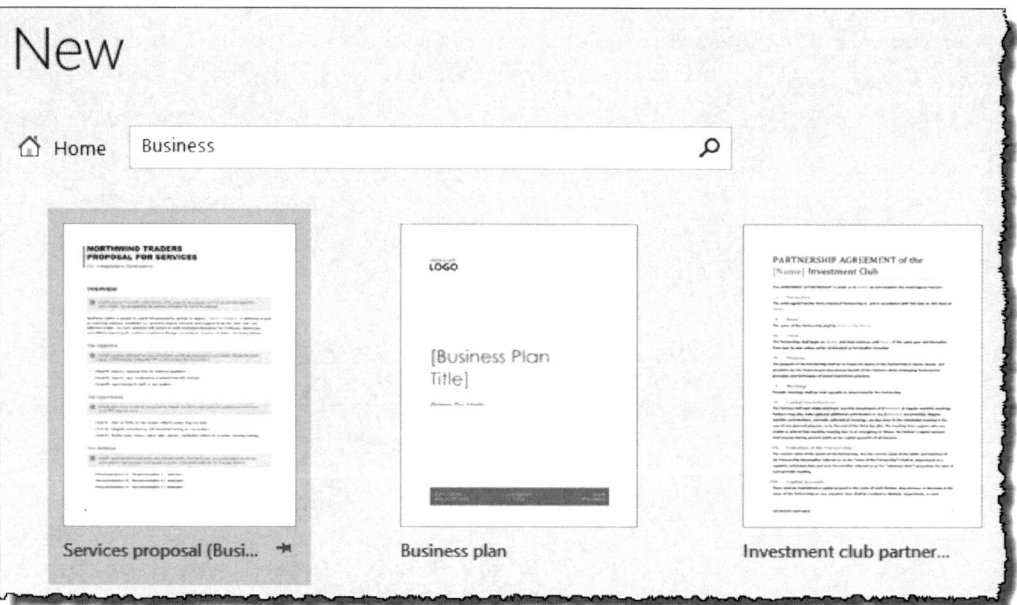

4. Select a template that you think might work.

    A preview is shown. You can click the arrow to the right of the preview to see previews of the next templates.

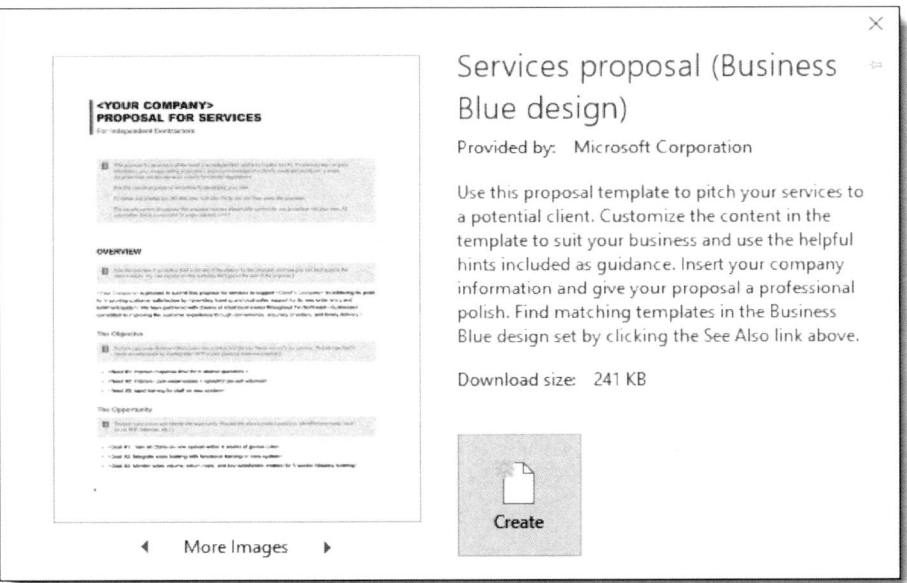

5. Click **Create**.

   A new document opens using the template.

Once you download a template, it will be available in your list of templates on the New screen.

Saving a document as a templates

In additional to basing documents on templates you find online, you can also create your own templates. Then, you can use them as the starting point for documents in the future. The templates you create will appear in the Personal category if you save them in the default templates folder.

1. Create a document with the elements and formatting you want in your template.
2. Click **File > Save As**.
   To open the Save As window.
3. In the "Save as type" list, click **Word Template**.
   Word will automatically change the active folder to Custom Office Templates. Unless you have a strong reason to do otherwise, you should save your templates here, because then they will appear on the New screen under the Personal category.
4. Enter a name for the template and click **Save**.

You will then be able to create new documents based on your template. Click **File > New**, click **Personal**, then click the template you want.

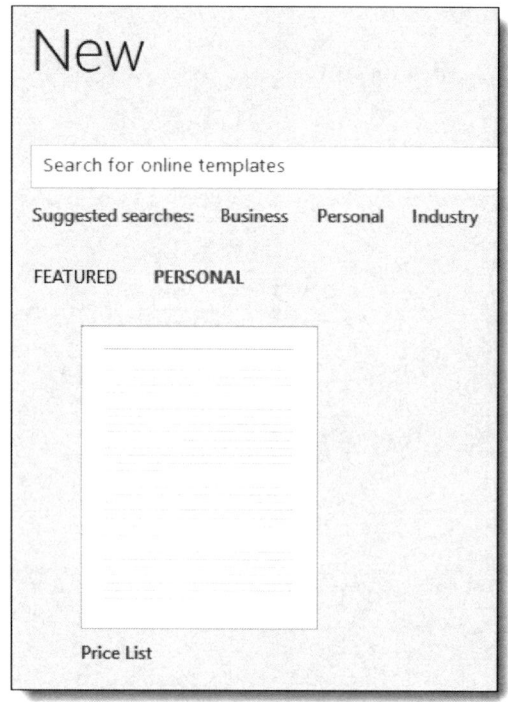

Exercise: Using templates

You need an Internet connection to complete some of these steps as written. You can still work with the local template file without an Internet connection.

 Exam Objective: MOS Word Core 1.1.2

Do This	How & Why
1. Click **File > New**.	To display the New screen in Backstage view. You see a list of Featured templates, and a search box.
2. Next to Suggested Searches, click **Business**.	You see a list of online templates you could download and use, along with a list of sub-categories on the right. Category Business 252 Small Business 206 Industry 85 Design Sets 59 Finance - Accounting 44
3. Click **Finance - Accounting**.	To view available templates.
4. Observer the previews of some of the available templates.	Click one to view the preview, then use the arrow to scroll through others.
5. Return to the document.	Press **Esc** to close the preview.

Do This	How & Why
6. Open Menu.	This document is a starting point for future Java Tucana menus. You will save it as a template.
7. Save the document as a template.	
a) Click **File > Save As**, then click **Browse**.	To open the **Save As** window.
b) In the "Save as type" list, click **Word Template**.	Notice that when you select the template file type, Word switches to the Custom Office Templates folder.
c) Click **Save**, then close the document.	
8. Create a new document based on your menu template.	
a) Click **File > New**.	There is now a Personal category in the New screen.
b) Click **Personal**, then click the **Menu** template.	A new document opens based on the template. Note that the document name (in the title bar) is not "Menu," but "Document" with a number.
9. Close the document without saving it.	

Assessment: Templates

1. Every Word document is based on a template. True or false?

   - True
   - False

2. What is the name of the template that opens when you first start Word? Choose the one correct answer.

   - Default
   - Basic
   - Blank
   - Normal

3. Which of the following are file extensions used for Word templates? Choose all the correct answers.

   - .dot
   - .wtm
   - .dotx
   - .wtmx

Summary: Document setup

You should now know how to:

- Change page layout options such as margins, page and line breaks, and hyphenation; create and control columns layouts; and insert new sections and show section numbers
- Use automatic spell checking or the Grammar and Spelling panes to proof documents, use AutoCorrect, and create an AutoCorrect entry
- Print documents, control print settings, add headers and footers, insert page numbers and dates in headers and footers, and use different first page or even and odd page headers and footers
- Use online templates, and create your own templates based on documents

Synthesis: Document setup

In this synthesis exercise, you will create a small baked goods menu, change layout settings, and add a header and a footer.

1. Open `Full Menu` and save it as `Full Menu Setup`.
2. Set the margins to moderate.
3. Use page breaks to put the Sandwiches and Soups of the Day sections on new pages.
4. For the Baked Goods items, set a right tab stop at 7 inches with a dot leader.
   It should look like this.

   ```
   BAKED·GOODS¶
   Bagel ----------------------------------------→--------------------------------------- $1¶
   Cheese·Danish ---------------------------------→------------------------------------ $1.50¶
   Doughnut --------------------------------------→------------------------------------ $1.25¶
   ```

5. Format the Sandwiches items in two columns.
6. For the Sandwiches items, add a right tab stop at 3.25 inches with a dot leader.
7. Add a column break before "Tucana Banana".
   It should now look like this.

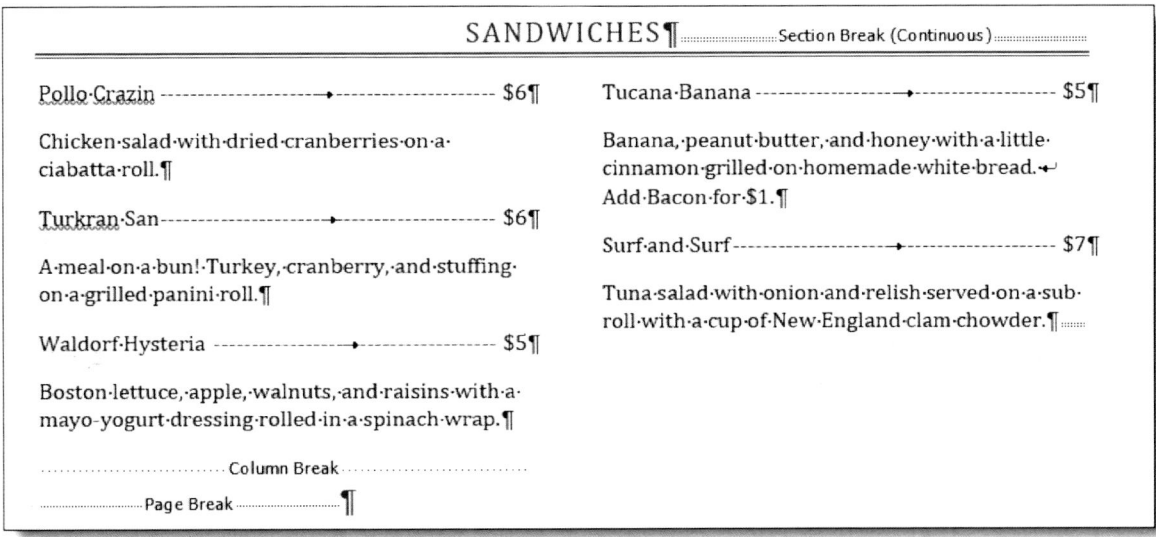

8. Format the Soups of the Day items the same as the Baked Goods.
   Try using the Format Painter.

9. Add a footer that looks like the following image.
   Hint: You can use the footer's default tab stops to right align the page numbers.

10. Add a Header that says `Java Tucana`, in Title style.

11. Make the first page have no header or footer.

12. Print preview the document.

13. Save and close the document.

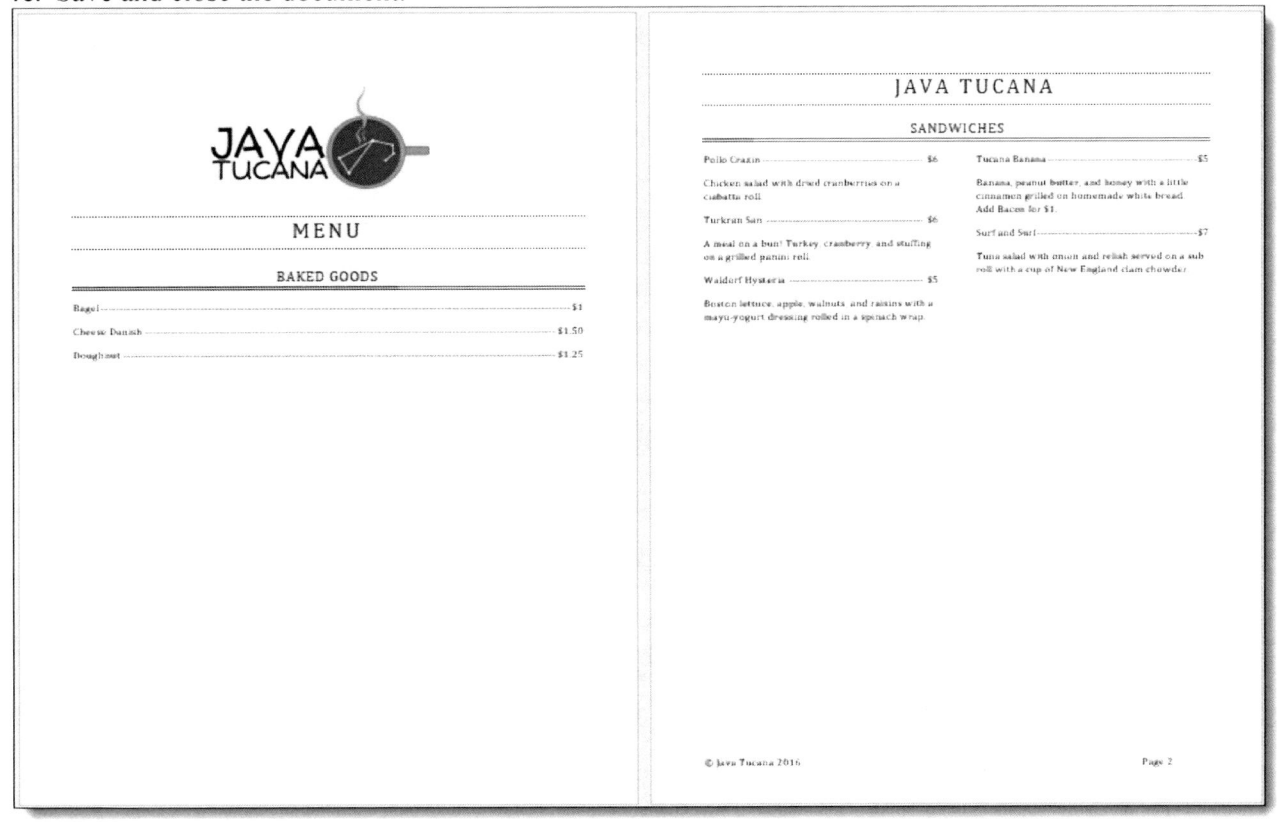

Chapter 4: Graphics

You will learn how to:

- Insert pictures
- Change picture layout
- Format pictures

Module A: Inserting pictures

There are several ways to insert pictures into a Word document, including pasting, opening a graphics file, and taking a screenshot.

You will learn how to:

- Insert graphics from files or the clipboard
- Insert screenshots
- Insert pictures from the web

Pictures in Word

There are several types of graphic elements you can add to Word documents. The term "picture" generally refers to graphics added from a file or the clipboard. Other graphics elements in Word include shapes, text boxes, SmartArt, WordArt, and charts.

Although pictures downloaded from the web and screen shots are inserted differently than most pictures, they are really graphics files, and once they are in a document, you format them as you would any other picture. One way to know if an object in Word is a picture is to select it. When a picture is selected, the Pictures Tools Format tab appears on the ribbon. The exact appearance of the tab you see might be different depending on your screen size.

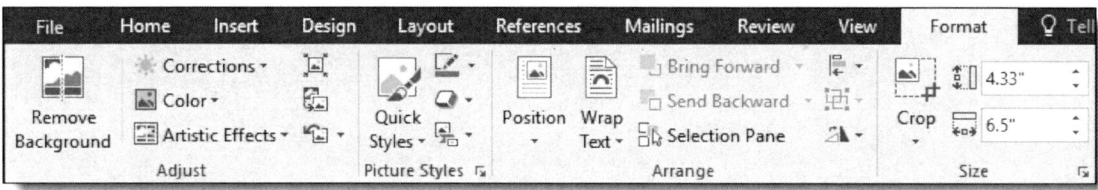

Inserting pictures

To insert a picture quickly, you can copy it from another source and paste it at the cursor, just as you would copy and paste text. You can also insert a picture from a file. Word recognizes many picture file formats.

 Exam Objective: MOS Word Core 5.1.2

1. Put the cursor where you want the picture.
    You can move and resize the picture later.
2. On the Insert tab, in the Illustrations group, click **Pictures**.
    The **Insert Picture** window opens.
3. If you want, select a file format from the file types list.
    If you need to narrow the search. By default, the window shows all supported graphics files.

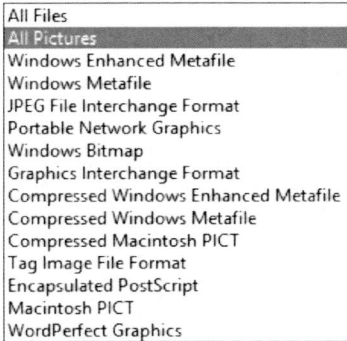

4. Select the file you want, and then click **Insert**.

   The window closes, and the picture is inserted into the document.

Inserting screen shots

Word allows you to insert a picture of an open window or part of your computer screen. Windows have to be open (not minimized) to be available for a screen shot.

 Exam Objective: MOS Word Core 5.1.3

1. Place the insertion point where you want the screenshot to appear.
2. On the Insert tab, click **Screenshot**.
   - To capture and place a shot of an open window, select it in the Screenshot gallery. You cannot take a screenshot of the Word window you are working in, but you can capture other open Word windows.

   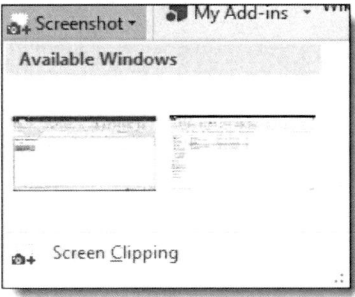

   - To select a section of your screen to capture, click **Screen Clipping**, then drag over the area of the screen you want to capture. Again, the current Word window is not visible for capture.

With either method, the screenshot is inserted at the point of the cursor.

Exercise: Inserting a picture

 Exam Objective: MOS Word Core 5.1.2, 5.1.3

Do This	How & Why
1. Start a new blank document, and save it as `Pics`.	Save it in the current chapter's data folder.
2. In Windows, click **Start**, type `paint`, and then press **Enter**.	To open the Paint program.
3. In Paint, open the image file `Table`.	From the current chapter's data folder.
4. Copy and paste the picture from Paint to Word: a) In Paint, on the Home tab, click **Select > Select All**. b) Press **Ctrl+C** c) Switch back to Pics, and press **Ctrl+V**.	 To paste the image into Word. This is one way to get graphics into a document: simply copy and paste them.
5. Press **Enter**.	To put the cursor below the image.
6. On the Insert tab, click **Pictures**.	The **Insert Picture** window opens.
7. In the data folder, select the file `CoffeeCup`, and then click **Insert**.	You could instead double-click the file. The picture is placed in the document.
8. Press the right arrow key, and then press **Enter**.	To place the cursor below the image.
9. On the Insert tab, click **Screenshot**.	You'll see thumbnail images of all open windows except that of the active document.
10. Click the thumbnail for the **Paint** window.	A screenshot of the Paint window is inserted, scaled to fit in the document.
11. Close Paint, and save and close Pics.	

Inserting pictures from the web

There is an online pictures browser built into Word. You can search for and insert pictures and graphics, and save them locally for future use.

1. On the Insert tab, in the Illustrations group, click **Online Pictures**.
   To open the **Insert Pictures** window. Note that you need to be connected to the Internet to search for online pictures.

   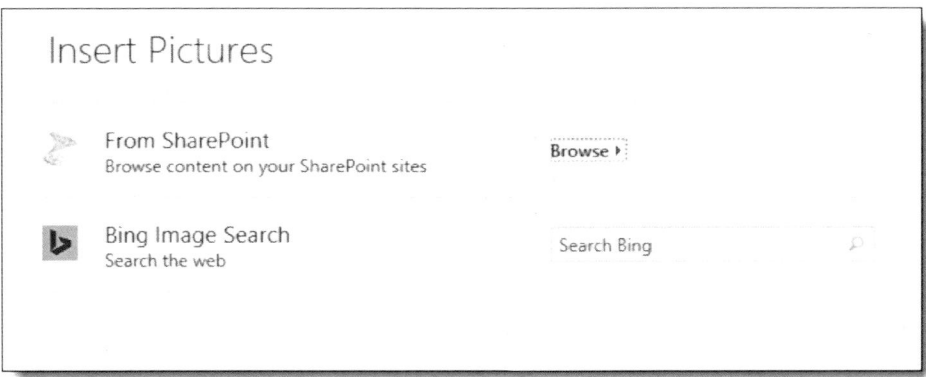

2. In the Bing Image Search box, type one or more search terms, and press **Enter**.
   To display your search results. By default, Bing shows you only images licensed under Creative Commons, meaning that you should be able to use them without any concern about rights.

3. Scroll through the images, click the one you want, then click **Insert**.
   It is downloaded and inserted into your document at the location of the cursor.

Exercise: Working with online images

An Internet connection is needed to search for images online.

Do This	How & Why
1. Open a new blank document, and save it as `Web Pic`.	
2. On the Insert tab, click **Online Pictures**.	The **Insert Pictures** window opens.
3. In the Bing Image Search box, type `coffee cup`, and then press **Enter**.	
4. In the search results, click any image you want.	To see information about the picture.
5. Click **Insert**.	It is inserted in the document.
6. Save and close the Web Pic document.	

Assessment: Inserting pictures

1. Which one of these is stored in a graphics file like other pictures?

   - Online pictures
   - Shapes
   - WordArt
   - SmartArt

2. A program window must be open (not minimized) to be captured by the Word Screenshot command. True or false?

   - True
   - False

Module B: Formatting pictures

When you want to do more than adjust a picture's size and place on the page, Word offers a number of formatting options to adjust color and contrast, apply artistic effects, and apply other visual effects, such as shadows, reflections, and soft edges.

You will learn how to:

- Make picture adjustments
- Apply artistic effects and picture styles
- Compress pictures in a document

Picture adjustments

You can adjust several visual features of a selected picture using the tools in the Adjust group on the Picture Tools Format tab. Any of these tools that has a gallery shows you small previews, and pointing to an option shows you a live preview in the document.

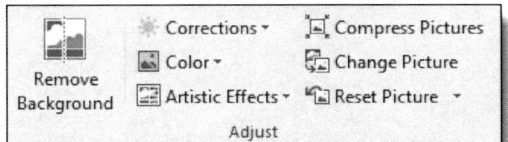

 Exam Objective: MOS Word Core 5.2.3

Remove Background	If the picture background is a smooth color with little variation (like a white background), this tool can replace it with a transparent area. You will be able to see text and the document background through the transparency, and text can be wrapped around the remaining image. The figure shows an image before and after removing the background.

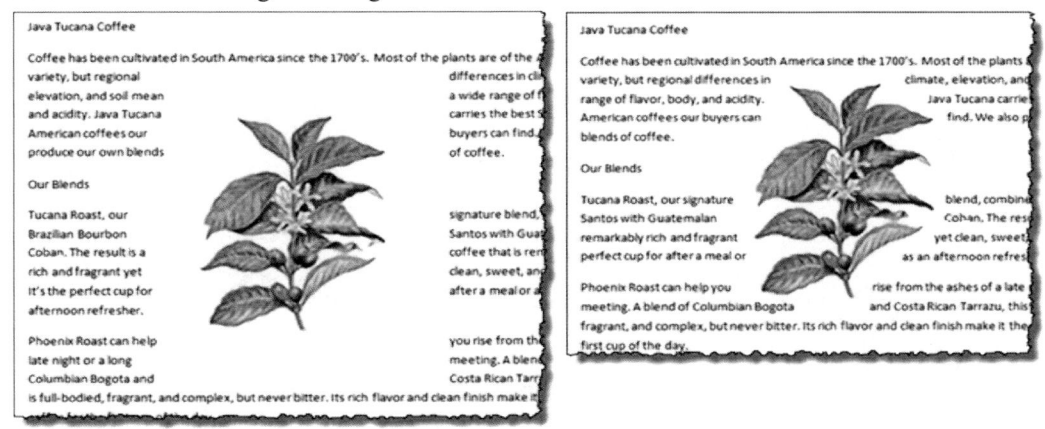

Corrections	Sharpen or soften image edges, and adjust contrast and brightness.
Color	Change color saturation and tone, or recolor the image.
Artistic Effects	These effects might make the picture look like a painting or a drawing, or make it blurry or granular, or look as though it's behind frosted glass.
Compress Pictures	This reduces the size of the picture data stored in the document, so that the overall document size is smaller.
Change Picture	Allows you to select a different image to go in the same place as the selected image.
Reset Picture	Removes adjustments and effects, and returns the image to its original state.

Applying effects

Artistic Effects is a tool that can alter a picture in a number of ways. For instance, it can make a picture look as if it's painted, drawn with a pencil, or being seen through frosted glass. Picture effects add to the outline or presentation of a picture as a whole, for example a beveled or drop-shadow look.

 Exam Objective: MOS Word Core 5.2.1, 5.2.2

1. Select the picture you want to modify.
    The Picture Tools Format tab appears.
2. On the Picture Tools Format tab, do one of the following.
    - In the Adjust group, click **Artistic Effects** to open the Artistic Effects gallery showing small previews. You can point to effects to see a live preview in the document. After you apply an artistic effect, you can change how it works by clicking **Artistic Effects** > **Artistic Effects**.

    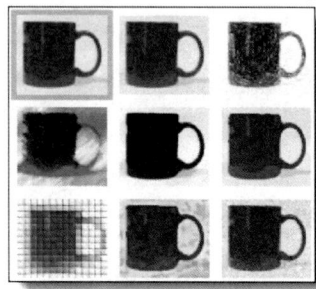

    - In the Picture Styles group, click **Picture Effects**, then one of the choices for an effect type to see a gallery of options. This figure shows some of the shadow options.

    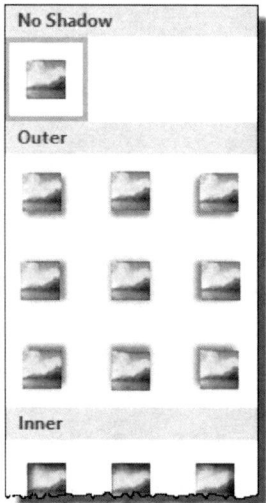

3. Click the effect you want to apply.
    The gallery closes, and the effect is applied.

Compressing pictures

When you insert a picture from the clipboard or a file, it is imported into the document at its full size and resolution. Its visible size is automatically reduced if the picture is too large for the document, but all the picture data are still there—even after you shrink or crop the picture. This can increase document file size considerably.

If smaller pictures and/or lower resolution are adequate for your project, and you are sure you won't need to undo any shrinking or cropping, then you can compress pictures to reduce your document's file size.

1. Select a picture.

   Any picture, unless you want to compress an individual picture, in which case, select that one.

2. On the Picture Tools Format tab, in the Adjust group, click **Compress Pictures**.

3. Select the compression options and output resolution.

   If you want to compress all pictures in the document, be sure to clear the **Apply only to this picture** check box.

4. Click **OK**.

5. Save to document.

   The reduced file size displays in Windows Explorer.

    Note: Once the document is saved and closed, the original picture information is lost and compression cannot be undone. You would have to re-insert the picture to return it to its original size and resolution.

Picture styles

A picture style is a set of picture effects applied at the same time. These effects do not change image values such as contrast, brightness, color, or artistic effects. Instead, picture styles affect and enhance the picture's presentation, including borders, drop shadows, reflections, beveling, and 3-D rotation.

 Exam Objective: MOS Word Core 5.2.5

You can experiment with these effects using the commands in the Picture Styles group on the Picture Tools Format tab.

To change individual effects, use the **Picture Border** and **Picture Effects** tools. As with other galleries, these show you small previews; pointing to a specific choice shows you a live preview in the document.

To apply picture styles to a selected picture, in the Picture Styles gallery, click the style. The figure here shows a picture with some effects applied; the picture on the right has a brown border, shadow, bevel, and 3-D rotation.

The Picture Layout command allows you to couple the picture with other graphical elements, such as shapes and text boxes.

The Format Picture pane

You might never need more than a few ribbon commands to format pictures in Word, but for more options and precision, you can use the Format Picture pane. To open it, right-click a picture, and click **Format Picture**. Here, various formatting options are in grouped categories.

 Exam Objective: MOS Word Core 5.2.4, 5.2.8

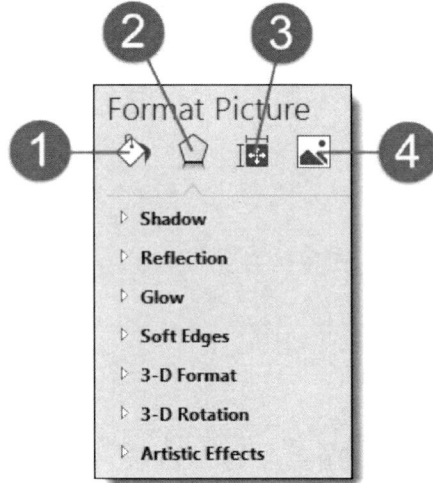

① *Fill & Line* options control the appearance of colors inside and along the border of the picture.

② *Effects* options control various effects.

③ *Layout and Properties* is for settings such as alignment and alternative text. To add alternative text to a graphic, which is important for accessibility, click this category, expand the Alt Text group, and enter a title and description of the graphic.

④ *Picture* settings allow you to control corrections, color, and cropping.

Many of the commands on the Picture Tools Format tab are also in the Format Picture pane. Here, you can precisely adjust settings for applied effects. You can also get to this window via the **Options** command at the bottom of most effects galleries.

Exercise: Formatting a picture

 Exam Objective: MOS Word Core 5.2.1, 5.2.2, 5.2.5, 5.2.8

Do This	How & Why
1. Open Logo, and save it as Logo Formatted.	The document contains a graphic of the Java Tucana logo.
2. Select the picture.	
3. On the Format tab, click **Corrections**, and under Brightness and Contrast, select the setting two options below the current (center) one.	To increase contrast 40%.

Do This	How & Why
4. On the Format tab, click **Artistic Effects**, and click **Cement**.	To apply a textured effect.
5. Point to different options in the Picture Styles gallery.	To see the live preview.
6. Experiment with picture effects like Shadow, Reflection, and 3-D Rotation.	In the Picture Style group, click **Picture Effects**, then try several of the galleries. If you want, you can click **Reset Picture** at any time to remove all effects and start over.
7. Add alternative text to the logo.	
a) Right-click the picture, then click **Format Picture**.	To display the Format Picture pane.
b) Click the Layout and Properties button.	To view layout and properties settings.
c) Add JT Logo as the Alt Text title.	Expand the Alt Text category, then type in the Title box.
d) Close the Format Picture pane.	Click its close button.
8. When you find an overall design you like, save and close the document.	

Assessment: Formatting pictures

1. If you crop a picture and then save and close the document, you can still recover the whole picture when you open the document again. True or false?

    - True
    - False

2. Which command removes effects and adjustments and returns a picture to its original state?

    - Remove Formatting
    - Reset Picture
    - Change Picture
    - No Style

Module C: Picture layout

Rarely do you insert a picture in Word and leave it as it is. In most cases, you want at least to adjust the image size and location, and the way text wraps around it.

You will learn how to:

- Adjust a picture's size and position
- Specify the way in which text wraps around a picture
- Add captions to pictures

Picture layout and formatting

When you select a picture in Word, the Picture Formatting tab becomes available. Many of the picture layout and formatting commands you need are on this tab. In general, layout refers to the way a picture is situated in the context of a document: its size, its place on the page, the way text wraps around it, and its caption. Formatting refers to adjusting a picture's visual qualities. These include adjustments in color and contrast, artistic effects, and special effects such as blur, shadow, framing, and 3-D rotation.

Manually changing size and position

By default, when you insert a picture in a Word document, it's treated as a character. That is, the picture appears at the cursor location, and text is wrapped around or pushed below it, as in this figure:

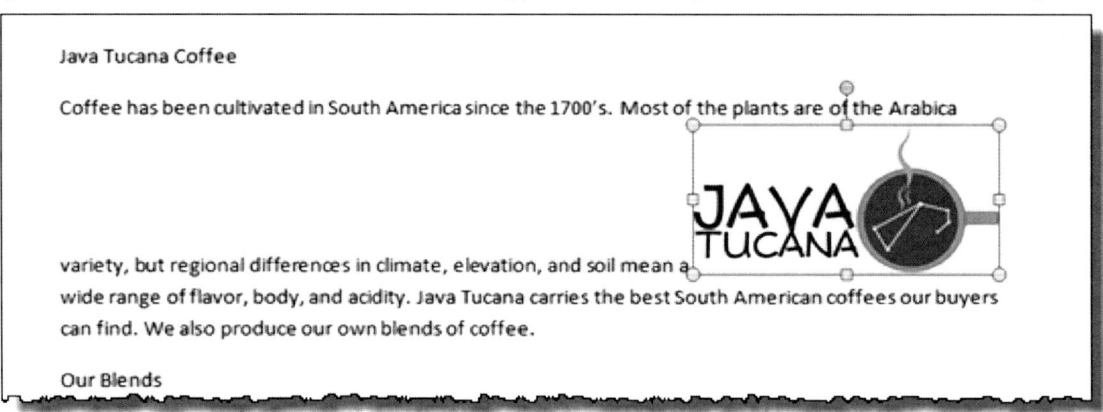

When you select a picture, a box appears around it with small circles and squares called *handles*. When you point to a handle, the cursor changes to reflect its function. You can use the handles to adjust the shape, size, and position of a selected picture.

 Exam Objective: MOS Word Core 5.2.4, 5.2.6, 5.2.7

- Drag a corner handle in or out to adjust the picture's size. This ensures that the ratio of height to width doesn't change.
- Drag the side handles in or out to change the width or height individually. This modifies the picture's shape from its original aspect ratio.
- Drag the top handle (the green circle) around to freely rotate the picture.
- Point inside the frame and drag the picture to a new location. It can be placed only where a character can, unless you change the Wrap Text setting. Then, you can drag it anywhere on the page.
- To crop a picture (cut off part of it), on the Picture Tools Format tab, click **Crop**. This will add cropping handles that you can drag to where you want.

Wrapping text around pictures

Exam Objective: MOS Word Core 5.2.6

After inserting a picture, you can change the way text flows around it. You can do this with the **Position** and **Wrap Text** commands on the Picture Tools tab, which appear only when a picture is selected. If a picture has transparent areas, wrapped text can flow into it. You can also place the picture behind or in front of the text, without changing its normal flow.

- Use the **Position** command to both place the picture on the page and wrap the text around it.
    Point to an option to see a live preview in your document.

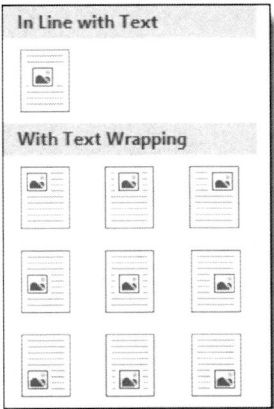

- Use the **Wrap Text** command to change only the way the text flows around the picture, but not the picture's position on the page.

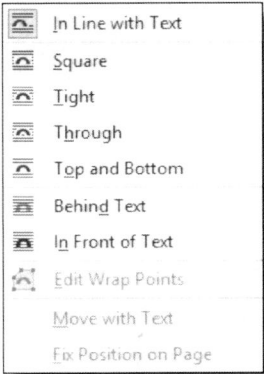

This command is also available from the shortcut menu when you right-click a picture. Once you change the style of text wrapping, you can drag the picture around to different positions. Before doing so, a picture is like a big character, and can be placed only in paragraphs.

- Another way to affect image position and text wrapping is through the Layout Options gallery.

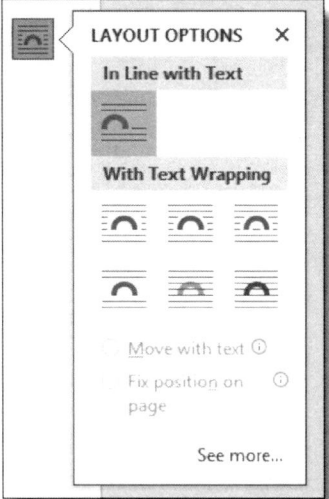

The Layout Options button appears to the right of a selected image. The Layout Options gallery contains some of the same layout and text-wrapping options as the Position and Wrap Text galleries. However, it's important to note that you can't preview the effects of selecting options by hovering over them in the Layout Options gallery.

The Layout window

 Exam Objective: MOS Word Core 5.2.7

You might never need more than a picture's handles and a few ribbon commands to arrange pictures in Word, but if you need more precision, you can use the **Layout** window. To open it, right-click a picture, and click **Size and Position**. If you choose a Text Wrapping option other than "In line with text," the options on the Position tab become available, giving you precise control over horizontal and vertical alignment, and the position of the graphic.

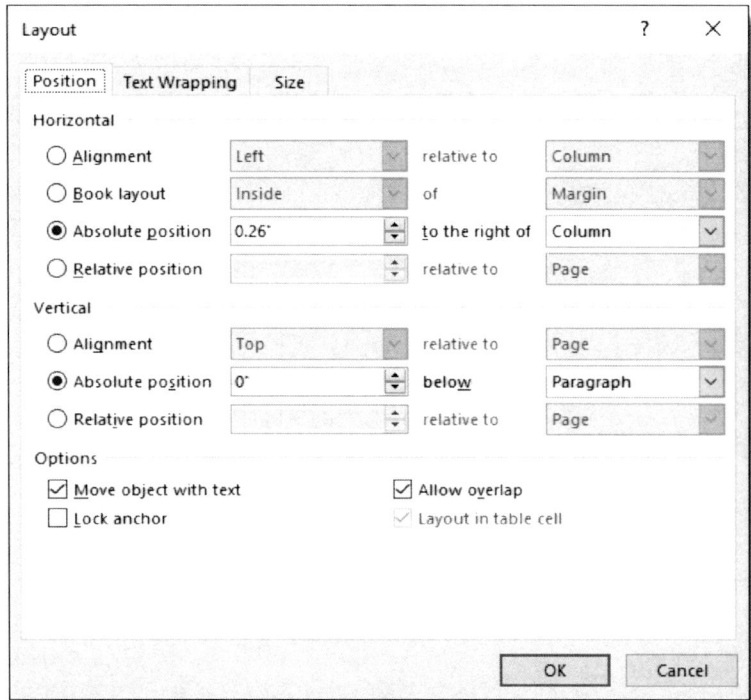

Adding captions to pictures

Adding a caption to a picture inserts a line of text and an automatic number in the Caption style. Captions are added the same way for most graphical objects, including pictures, shapes, WordArt, SmartArt, and clip art.

Exam Objective: MOS Word Expert 3.2.2

1. Right-click the picture, and click **Insert Caption**.
   To open the Caption window.

   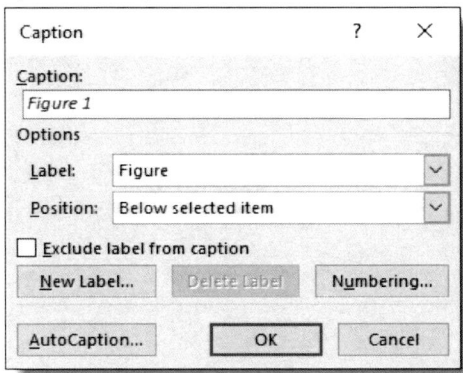

2. You can leave the default label as-is, or set any caption options you want:
   - Add a caption to the label.
   - Change the label to **Equation**, **Figure**, or **Table**.
   - Position the caption above or below the picture.
   - Exclude the label (the number will remain).
   - Create a new label to add to the list.
   - Change the numbering style.

3. Click **OK**.

   Figure 1: The Blue Mug

   The caption is added above or below the picture.

Note that the caption is not functionally tied to the picture, and can be either moved or deleted individually. If you change the order of captions, you'll have to update fields for the numbers to display in order again. To do this, press **Ctrl+A** to select all text, and then press **F9**.

Exercise: Changing picture layout

 Exam Objective: MOS Word Core 5.2.3, 5.2.4, 5.2.7

Do This	How & Why
1. Open `Blue Brew`, and save it as `New Blue Brew`.	In the current chapter's data folder.
2. Click the picture to select it.	Handles appear around the picture to indicate that it is selected.
3. Drag any corner handle to the center of the image.	To shrink it. 
4. Remove the background from the image. a) On the Format tab, click **Remove Background**. b) Drag out the border in the pink area to show the whole cup. c) Click **Keep Changes**.	
5. Right-click the image, and click **Wrap Text > Tight**.	
6. Drag the image to the lower left of the text.	Adjust it until you like the results. It should look something like the image below.
7. Save and close the document.	

Assessment: Picture layout

1. Which method will preserve aspect ratio when you resize a picture?

    - Hold down Shift when you resize it.
    - Right-click and drag the side handles.
    - Drag a corner handle.
    - Check Lock Aspect Ratio on the Format tab.

2. To be able to drag a picture around more freely, change its Text Wrap setting to anything other than In Line with Text. True or false?

    - True
    - False

3. A picture caption is grouped with the picture, so if you move one, the other will move. True or false?

    - True
    - False

Summary: Graphics

You should now know how to:

- Insert pictures, screenshots, and online images in your documents
- Adjust picture settings, add effects, apply picture styles, compress pictures, and use the Format Picture pane to control various aspects of pictures and to add alternative text
- Change picture size and position, wrap text around graphics, and add captions to them

Synthesis: Graphics

1. Open `JT Services`, and save it as `JT Services Pic`.
2. Insert the picture `JT-Logo`.
3. Reduce the picture to about a quarter of its original size, maintaining its aspect ratio.
4. Change the Text Wrap setting to **Square**.
5. Drag the logo to the upper-right so it is to the right of the first two headings.
6. Using options on the format tab, apply any effect you want to the logo.
    You might need to readjust its position, depending on what effects you apply.
7. Insert the picture `CoffeeTime`.
8. Change the Text Wrap to **Tight**, and drag the picture to the location shown in the figure.
9. Remove the background, so the text wraps more closely to the image.
10. When the document looks good to you, save and close it.

Your document should look something like this after this exercise.

The document with graphics inserted and formatted

Chapter 5: Tables

You will learn how to:

- Insert tables in a document
- Format tables

Module A: Creating tables

Tables in Word can be used for a number of things, including lists of data, calendars, checklists, and layout structure. Anything you put in your documents can also go in a table, such as text, numbers, shapes and pictures, and even another table. You can create a simple blank table, draw a table, convert a selection of text into a table, or make use of one of the built-in tables that come with Word.

You will learn how to:

- Insert a table
- Use the Draw Table tool
- Insert Quick Tables
- Convert text into a table

Tables

Tables are rows and columns of information. Each juncture of a row and column is called a *cell*, and this is where data are stored.

Tables can have header rows and/or header columns to describe the information, as shown in the figure. This table of information about the Greek alphabet is included with Word as a Quick Table.

Letter name	Uppercase	Lowercase	Letter name	Uppercase	Lowercase
Alpha	A	α	Nu	N	ν
Beta	B	β	Xi	Ξ	ξ
Gamma	Γ	γ	Omicron	O	o
Delta	Δ	δ	Pi	Π	π
Epsilon	E	ε	Rho	P	ρ
Zeta	Z	ζ	Sigma	Σ	σ
Eta	H	η	Tau	T	τ
Theta	Θ	θ	Upsilon	Υ	υ
Iota	I	ι	Phi	Φ	φ
Kappa	K	κ	Chi	X	χ
Lambda	Λ	λ	Psi	Ψ	ψ
Mu	M	μ	Omega	Ω	ω

In this example, there is an external border, but no visible internal borders, so the data looks like a tabular list. There are many options for setting borders in rows, columns, and cells. Borders refer to lines that are visible on screen and that will print. If you want to see the grid lines (or not) while you are working on a table with no borders, you can click **View Gridlines** on the Layout tab. This makes the same example look like this:

Letter name	Uppercase	Lowercase
Alpha	A	α
Beta	B	β
Gamma	Γ	γ
Delta	Δ	δ
Epsilon	E	ε
Zeta	Z	ζ

Gridlines are visible while you are working, but they don't print.

Inserting simple tables

There are two ways to insert a simple, blank table.

Exam Objective: MOS Word Core 3.1.3

- On the Insert tab, click **Table**, then click on the grid.

    To insert a table with corresponding dimensions. Rows will be one line high and columns will be evenly spaced. The table will take up the width of the page. Formatting can be adjusted after the table is in place.

    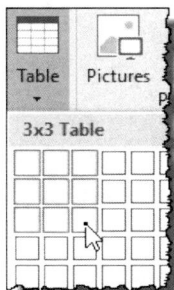

- Click **Table** > **Insert Table**.

    To open the **Insert Table** window. Here, you can specify the number of rows and columns, and set column width and AutoFit behavior. Click **OK** to insert the table.

    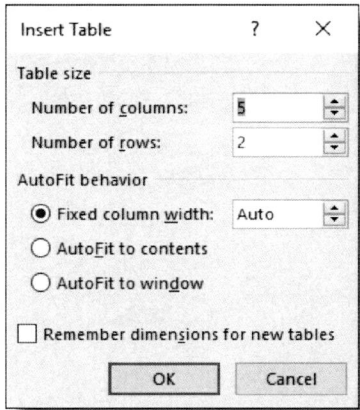

Drawing tables

Drawing a table allows you a little more control and is suitable for tables with irregular dimensions.

1. On the Insert tab, click **Tables** > **Draw Table**.

    The pointer looks like a pencil, and the Table Tools Design tab is available.

2. Drag to draw lines and boxes.

    - Drag straight across or up and down to draw lines.

    - Drag diagonally to draw a box. You can draw individual cells or draw bigger boxes and draw lines within it.

        Continued...

- Drawn tables don't have to be regular or symmetrical.
- To remove a line you don't want, click **Eraser** on the Table Tools Design tab. The pointer changes into an eraser. Click on lines to remove them, or drag over areas to remove areas of a table or the whole table.

3. To exit the tool, press **Esc** or click anywhere outside the table.

    You can use the table drawing and erasing tools on any existing tables, not just on those that were drawn in the first place.

Using tables for layout

We often think of tables as containers for lists of data, such as employee information or sales data, but tables in Word can also be used to control page layout. For example, if you want to create a one-page company newsletter, you could create a table that takes up the whole page, and then use cells to contain text and graphics. This way, paragraphs and pictures stay in place and are not easily shifted by other things moving on the page.

The table drawing tool is especially useful for drawing irregular tables like the one in the figure, which could be used to control page layout. Word has many options for manipulating a table once it is in place. For instance, you can insert, remove, and resize rows and columns; merge and split cells; define a header row; and sort table content.

Quick Tables

Quick Tables are already formatted and in some cases populated with sample data. For instance, calendar Quick Tables have a month name and dates entered, so you can get some idea of how it might look. After inserting one of these, you can delete the data and enter the month and dates you need.

On the Insert tab, click **Table > Quick Tables** to display the Quick Tables gallery, then choose the one you want.

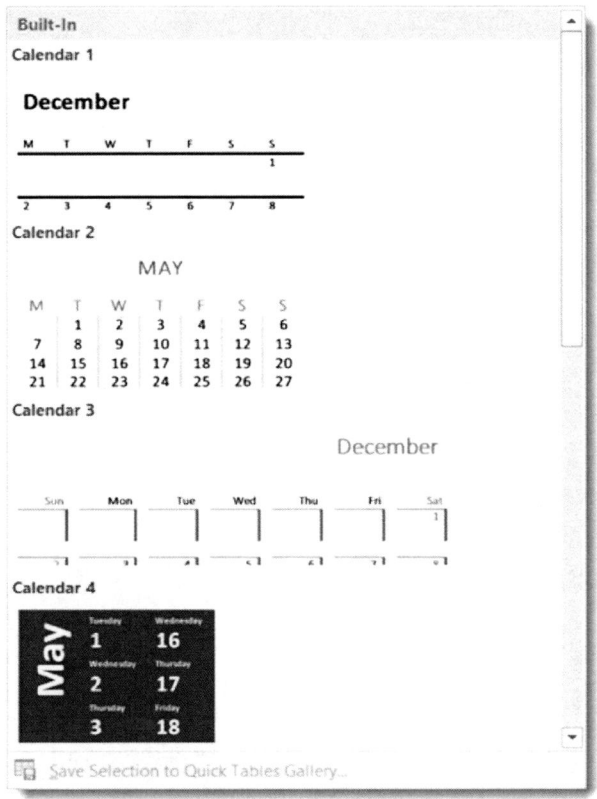

One of the most useful features of Quick Tables is the ability to add your own tables to the gallery. After you create and format your own table, click **Save Selection to Quick Tables Gallery** (at the bottom of the gallery). Your table is then available in the gallery.

Exercise: Creating tables

 Exam Objective: MOS Word Core 3.1.3

Do This	How & Why
1. Start a new, blank document in Word.	
2. On the Insert tab, click **Table**.	To display the Insert Table grid.
3. Click the 4x6 location on the grid.	To insert a table that's four columns by six rows.
4. On the Table Tools Layout tab, click **Draw Table**.	
5. Experiment with the Draw Table tool: • Drag to draw a large box. • Draw lines inside the box for columns and rows. • Try irregular rows or cells that don't span the whole table.	
6. Experiment with the **Eraser** tool: • Click on a single line to remove it. • Drag over areas to remove several lines.	
7. Use the **Eraser** tool to remove all of the tables on the page.	You should now be back to a blank page.
8. On the Insert tab, click **Table > Insert Table**.	To open the **Insert Table** window.
9. Set the table options: a) Set columns to 4 and rows to 6. b) Select **Fixed column width** and set it to 1". c) Click **OK**.	The table is added with 1-inch columns. The cursor is in the first cell.
10. On the Table Tools Layout tab, click **Delete > Delete Table**.	You are back to a blank page.

Do This	How & Why
11. On the Insert tab, click **Table > Quick Tables**.	To open the built-in tables gallery.
12. Click the table of your choice.	To add it to the document.
13. Close the document without saving.	Leave Word open.

Converting text to table

You might decide that existing content would look better or be better organized in a table.

 Exam Objective: MOS Word Core 3.1.1, 3.1.2

1. Select the text you want to put in a table.
2. On the Insert tab, click **Table > Convert Text to Table**.
   To open the **Convert Text to Table** window.

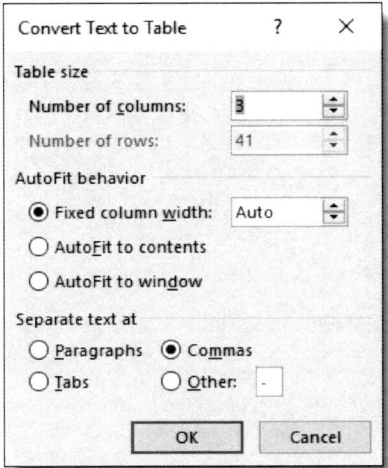

3. Set options, if necessary.
   - Word guesses an appropriate table size according to the text selected. You can change it, but choices are limited by what's selected.
   - Word also guesses the *delimiter* that separates units of data to go into different cells.
4. Click **OK**.
   The table is inserted and the selected text moved into it. You can adjust and edit this table just as you would any other.

To reverse the process and convert a table to text, select the table, then click **Convert to Text** on the Table Tools Layout tab.

Exercise: Converting a list into a table

 Exam Objective: MOS Word Core 3.1.1

Do This	How & Why
1. Open `Coffee List` and save it as `Coffee Table`.	In the current chapter's data folder. This document contains a list of coffee origins and types. The two pieces of information are separated by a tab character.
2. Select the tabular list.	
3. On the Insert tab, click **Table > Convert Text to Table**.	The **Convert Text to Table** window opens.
4. Select **AutoFit to Contents**.	Notice that Tabs is selected under "Separate text at." Word recognized the tab characters in the selected text.
5. Click **OK**.	The table is created with columns that are just wide enough to contain the contents.
6. Save and close the file.	

Assessment: Creating tables

1. Gridlines show you where table borders are, but they do not print. True or false?
    - True
    - False

2. Which tool is best for creating a table with irregular rows, columns, and cells?
    - Insert Table window
    - Draw Table tool
    - Quick Tables
    - Insert Table grid

3. The table eraser tool can only be used on tables created with the table drawing tool. True or false?
    - True
    - False

Module B: Formatting tables

Once a table is in place, you can format it in many ways. You can resize the whole table or individual rows and columns. You can apply background shading and borders in different colors. You can also define headers for each column and sort the table on column data.

You will learn how to:

- Resize tables
- Add, remove, and move rows and columns
- Define a header row
- Sort a table

Table formatting

When you select all or part of a table, or when the cursor is in a table, these Table Tools tabs appear: Design and Layout. The Design tab allows you to add shading and borders and apply table styles. It also has the table drawing tools. The Layout tab provides commands to manipulate rows, columns, and cells, as well as data alignment and sorting.

Exam Objective: MOS Word Core 3.1.4

The Table Styles section on the Table Tools Design tab allows you to pick a pre-defined table format from a gallery. Styles include borders, shading, and header highlighting.

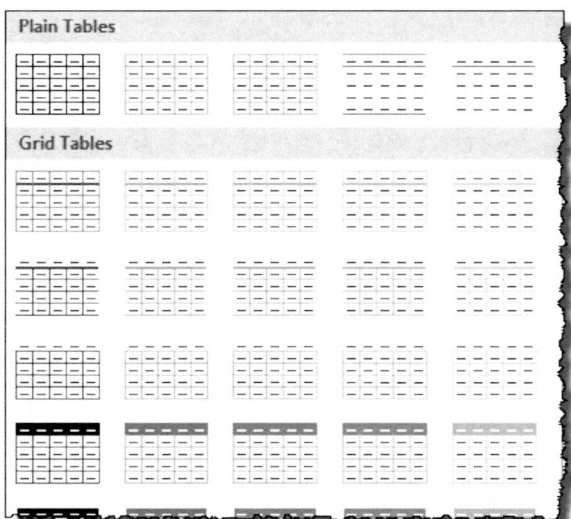

You can also set borders and shading individually for parts of a table by using those buttons on the Table Tools Design tab. For instance, you could select a cell or range of cells and apply a thick border around them for emphasis.

Resizing tables

There are a number of ways to manually or automatically control and change the size of rows, columns, and tables.

 Exam Objective: MOS Word Core 3.2.3, 3.2.4, 3.2.5

- On the Table Tools Layout tab, click **AutoFit**, and then click an option.
- To change the size of rows or columns, drag the borders to where you want them.
    Where you can drag a border might be restricted by what you've selected, cell content, page size, and table settings. When you drag a column border in selected rows, the column width changes only in the selected rows. Thus, you can also select a single row and drag the border of one of its cells to change its margins.

    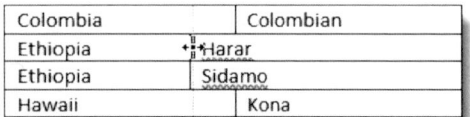

- To merge multiple cells into one, select two or more adjacent cells, right click them, and then click **Merge**.
- To split a cell, right-click in it, and click **Split Cells**. Set the number of rows and columns into which to split them, then click **OK**.
- To split a table in two, click within the row you want to be first in the split table, then click **Split Table** on the Table Tools Layout tab.
- To distribute rows or columns evenly, select all or a range of rows and/or columns, right-click, and click **Distribute Rows Evenly** or **Distribute Columns Evenly**.
- To specify row and column size, set the values on the Row and Column tabs of the **Table Properties** window.
- To specify cell/column margins, first display the ruler, if necessary (on the View tab, click **Ruler**); click in the cell/column you wish to adjust; and on the ruler, drag the left- and right-edge column handles for that cell/column to reduce or enlarge its width. Or, on the Table Tools Layout tab, in the Cell Size group, click in the Table Column Width box, and specify the size numerically.

Manipulating rows and columns

Although there are many commands on the Table Tools tabs, most of what you want to do can be done from the menu that opens when you right-click a table.

- For some operations, you need to select a column, row, cell, or range of cells first:
    - To select a column, point above it, and click when you see a heavy down arrow.

    - To select a row, click in the margin to the left of it.
    - To select a cell, triple-click in it.
    - To select a range of cells, drag over them the way you would to select text.
- There are a couple of ways to add a new row or columns.

- Right-click the existing row or column where you want to add another, then click **Insert**, and click the option you want. You can instead use the insert options on the Layout tab. If you right-click on a value in a cell, you might get a different menu.
- Select a row, then point in the margin just above or below the selected row and click the plus sign that appears. The same mouse-based method works for columns.

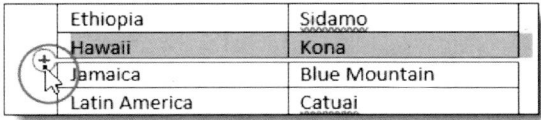

- To move rows or columns, select the row or column you want to move, then drag it to the location you want.

  Be careful about where you actually release the mouse button.

- To delete rows or columns, select the row(s) or column(s) you want to delete, right-click the selected item(s), and then click **Delete Rows** or **Delete Columns**.

  Pressing the **Delete** key just deletes the data, leaving the cells empty.

Defining a header row

If you have column headings in the first row of a table, and that table might be split across two or more pages, you might want to repeat the header at the top of each new page.

Exam Objective: MOS Word Core 3.2.6

1. Click in any cell in the first row.

   You can define only the first row as a header row.

2. On the Table Tools Layout tab, click **Repeat Header Rows**.

   You can also do this from the Row tab in the **Table Properties** window.

   This defines the first row as a header row, and repeats that row if the table is split across two or more pages.

Specifying a table title

You can specify a table title and description in the **Table Properties** window. Doing so provides a text representation of the table (or other object), known as *Alt Text*. This can be helpful as a clarifying description of the table and its contents. It's also helpful to those with visual disabilities.

1. With the table selected, click **Properties**.

   On the Table Tools Layout tab, in the Table group.

   The **Table Properties** window opens.

2. Display the Alt Text tab.

3. Specify a table title.

   In the Title box. You can also describe the table in the Description box.

   Continued...

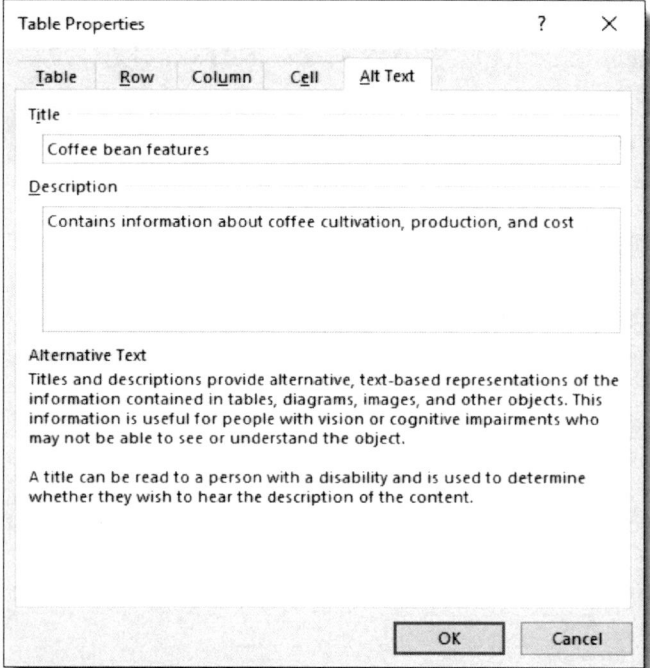

4. Click **OK**.

Sorting table content

You can sort a table on one or more columns. If there is a header row defined, the column names appear in the sort options. If not, columns are designated as Column 1, Column 2, and so on.

Exam Objective: MOS Word Core 3.2.1

1. Click in any cell.
    To put the cursor in the table and make the table tools available. You can also select a column, or a range of rows, if you plan to sort only that column or range.
2. On the Table Tools Layout tab, click **Sort**.
    To open the **Sort** window.

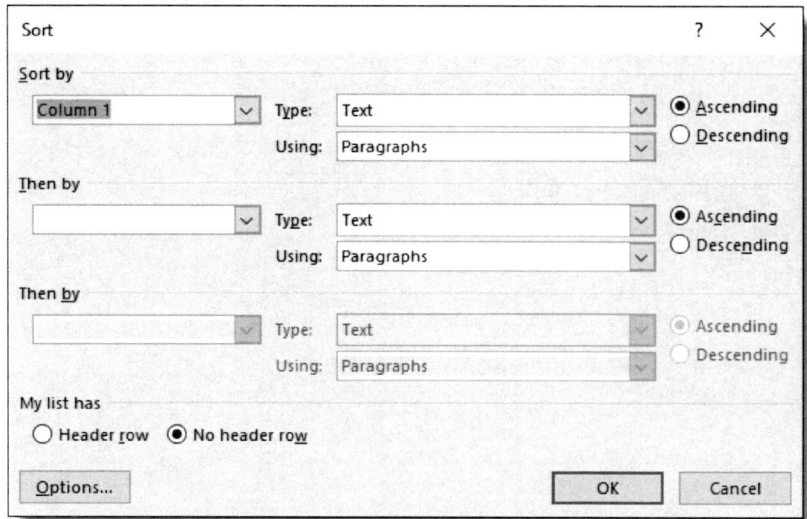

3. Set the sorting options, if necessary:

- Select a column to sort on. If you have defined a header row, you see column headers in the list. Otherwise, columns are numbered.
- You can select a second column to sort on, if you want. For instance, in a table of names, you might sort by last name, and then by first name.
- If your first row is headers, be sure to select **Header row**, so that these values don't get sorted in with the data.
- The **Options** button opens the **Sort Option** window, providing a few more settings, such as language, and whether to sort the selected column only.

4. Click **OK**.

   The table is sorted by the information in the column(s) you selected. By default, the data in each row stays together. For instance, if you sort employee records by last name, the employee first name and contact information stays with the last name. Sometimes you might want to sort only the selected column, and you can choose that option in the **Sort Options** window.

Exercise: Formatting and sorting a table

Exam Objective: MOS Word Core 3.2.1, 3.2.4, 3.2.6

Do This	How & Why
1. Open `Region Table`, and save it as `Region-Variety Table`.	
2. Drag the border between the two columns to the left.	To make just the first column narrower.
3. Double-click the border between the columns.	To "best fit" the first column, making it just wide enough to fit the longest text it contains.
4. On the Layout tab, click **AutoFit > AutoFit Contents**.	To fit the all the data better.
5. Select the bottom two rows.	The micro formatting toolbar is displayed.
6. Click **Delete > Delete Rows**.	
7. Select the top row. On the micro formatting toolbar, click **Insert > Insert Above**.	

Do This	How & Why
8. In the top row, enter the values `Region` and `Variety`.	
9. With the cursor in the first row, on the Table Tools Layout tab, in the Data group, click **Repeat Header Rows**.	To define it as a header row.
10. Also in the Data group, click **Sort**.	The **Sort** window opens, with Region in the "Sort by" field.
11. In the "Then by" list, click **Variety**.	
12. Click **OK**.	The table is sorted first by region, then by variety name. If you look at the Latin American varieties, this will be clear.
13. Save and close the file.	

Assessment: Formatting tables

1. By default, sorting a table on a column will sort only that column, leaving data in the other columns in place. True or False?

    - True
    - False

2. To delete a column, select it and press Delete. True or false?

    - True
    - False

3. Besides the Insert Table window, where can you find AutoFit options for a table?

    - Design tab
    - Table Tools Layout tab
    - Right-click menu
    - Table Properties

Summary: Tables

You should now know how to:

- Insert simple tables and quick tables, draw tables, and convert text into a table
- Format a table by resizing, manipulate rows and columns, define a header row, and sort table data

Synthesis: Tables

In this synthesis exercise, you'll open a document with a list of customer information, convert it to a table, manipulate its data, and format it using a style.

1. Open `Customer List`, and save it as `Customer Table`.
2. Convert that tabular list to a table.
   AutoFit the contents. Don't include the title.
3. Add a header row with the values `Customer`, `Rep`, and `Region`.
4. Define the first row as a header row.
5. Move the first column to make it the last column.
   Select the column, and drag it right.
6. Sort the table by **Rep**.
7. On the Design tab, apply a table style of your choosing.
   You might want to clear the **First Column** check box in the Table Style Option group.

The result should look something like the figure below, depending on which style you picked.

The customer list turned into a formatted table

Java Tucana Customer List

Rep	Region	Customer
Blackwell	International	The Grand
Daniels	US	BlazerFire
Daniels	US	CrossCountry Airways
Franklin	Eurozone	Central
Franklin	Eurozone	Imagenie
Franklin	Eurozone	YourWay Airline
Hernandez	Eurozone	Earth Farm
Hernandez	Eurozone	Gleeson Associates
Hernandez	Eurozone	Red Rock Mountain Tours

Alphabetical Index

Alt Text...129
    Creating..129
Alternative text..110
Attributes...28, 32
    Character..28
    Paragraph...32
AutoCorrect...79, 80
    Creating entries...80
    Exceptions..79
    Setting options..79
Backstage view..6
Breaks...69
    Columns..69
Bullets...53, 54
    Using pictures as..54
    Using symbols as..53
Captions for pictures...................................115
Character attributes.......................................28
Clear formatting..48
Clipboard..17
Closing documents...7
Columns..68, 69
    About...68
    Breaks..69
    Creating..68
    Setting up...68
Copying text..17
Creating new documents..............................11
Cutting text..17
Date and time..88
    In header or footer....................................88
Default options...76
    Proofing...76
Dialog box launcher...4
Document views...22
Documents......................6, 7, 11, 12, 22, 23
    Closing...7
    Creating..11
    Opening..6
    Saving..12
    Switching between....................................23
    Viewing side by side.................................23
    Views..22
Format Painter..29
Format Picture pane.....................................110
Format Picture window...............................110
Formatting..28, 32
    Characters..28
    Paragraphs...32
Grammar..75, 77
    Checking..75
    Proofing options..77
    Settings...77
    Style...77
Headers and footers...............85, 86, 87, 88, 89
    Adding date and time..............................88
    Adding page numbers..............................86
    Built-in..89

Formatting page numbers............................87
Headers and footers......................................90
    Different first page....................................90
    Different odd and even pages...............90
Hyphenation..65
Indents..36
Line breaks...64
Line numbers...66
Line spacing...34
Lists..51, 53, 56
    Controlling numbering............................56
    Creating..51
    Formatting...53
    Promoting, demoting items....................53
Margins...63
Non-breaking spaces.....................................64
Numbered lists..56
    Controlling..56
Numbering...56
    Changing format.......................................56
Online Pictures..105
Opening a document......................................6
Options..79
    AutoCorrect..79
Page breaks..64
Page layout..62
Page numbers...86, 87
    Formatting...87
Pagination..66
Paragraph attributes......................................32
Pasting text..18
Pictures......102, 103, 107, 108, 109, 110, 112, 113, 114, 115
    Adding captions to..................................115
    Artistic effects..108
    Compressing...108
    Formatting..110, 112
    Inserting..102
    Layout window..114
    Screenshots..103
    Size and position....................................112
    Styles..109
    Wrapping text around...........................113
Pictures web..105
Printing...83, 84
    Print settings..84
Proofing...76
    Setting options..76
Quick Access toolbar.................................4, 8
    Customizing..8
Quick Styles...46
Quick Tables..123
Ribbon...4
Saving documents..12
Screenshots...103
Sections...71
    About...71
    Working with..71

Alphabetical Index

Selecting text 16
Spelling 75
    Checking 75
Split document window 22
Starting Word 5
Status bar 4
Style sets 47
Styles 46
    Character 46
    Paragraph 46
Symbols 11
    Inserting 11
Table 129
    Description 129
    Title 129
Tables 120, 121, 122, 125, 127, 128, 129, 130
    Converting text to 125
    Converting to text 125
    Drawing 121
    Formatting 127
    Header row 129
    Inserting 121
    Manipulating columns 128

Manipulating rows 128
Resizing 128
Sorting content 130
To control layout 122
Tabs 38, 39, 42, 43
    Clearing stops 43
    Leaders 43
    Setting in Tab window 42
    Setting on the ruler 39
    Stop types 39
Templates 93, 94, 95
    From the web 94
    Local 95
Text 16
    Manipulating 16
Themes 46, 47
Undo command 18
Views 22
Widow/orphan control 66
Word 5
    Starting 5
Wrapping text 113
Zoom options 23